425 Ways

to

Stretch Your $$$$

To Joe & Christina

Happy Saving

Vernon Will

20 07

Congratulations
on your
marriage.

Other books by Vernon L. Williams

o *Paddle Your Own Boat: 10 Rules that Guarantee Career Success*

o *Why Employees Fail to Meet Performance Expectations & How to Fix the Problem*

Available at **www.vernonwilliams.net**

425 Ways

to

Stretch Your $$$$

VERNON L. WILLIAMS

Library of Congress Cataloging-in-Publication Data

Williams, Vernon L.

425 Ways to Stretch Your $$$$ / Vernon L. Williams

Includes bibliographical references and index.
ISBN 0-9777338-4-X

Published by Empowerment Publishers

This book is available at special quantity discounts to use as premiums and sales promotion, or for use in corporate or government training programs. For more information please visit **www.vernonwilliams.net.**

Dedication

This book is dedicated with love and affection to my wife, Gayle, who gives me love and encouragement every day.

Acknowledgements

Although most people do not rush to read the acknowledgements, it is a terrific opportunity for the author to express sincere appreciation to the special people who helped make the project possible.

My sincere gratitude goes to my wife Gayle who provided steadfast encouragement, served as a "Sanity-Tester", designed the book cover and served as a proofreader.

Thank you to my good friend and brother in Christ, Stephen Gallison, who gave me the idea to write a book.

Thanks to Tom Wemett, immediate past president of the National Association of Exclusive Buyer Agents, who reviewed a portion of the manuscript.

Thanks also go out to my "two mothers-in-law" Mrs. Elizabeth Budd and Mrs. Martina Beckett, who have always supported and encouraged me in everything I have done.

Finally, thanks to Kathryn Troutman and Michel Dopson who so generously shared their publishing knowledge and experience.

Contents

Preface

A research organization was taking a poll to find out how families spend their money.

Researcher: Sir, could you tell me how you spend your income?

Interviewee: I spend my money as follows:

30% food
30% clothing
40% shelter
20% everything else

Researcher: My goodness!! That is 120%.

Interviewee: I know. And it gets worse every year.

Maybe you do not spend 120% of your income, but that exchange reminds me of some rather startling statistics I read recently:

Despite a median income of $63,000 for a two-income household, more than 63 percent of America's workers live paycheck-to-paycheck.

—American Payroll Association

20% of employees say they are unable to carry on normal work activities three days per week due to financial concerns.

—Public Agenda poll

Nearly half (46%) of all Americans have less than $10,000 saved for their retirement.

—Public Agenda poll

When a group of parents with children under 18 was asked how much they were saving for college nearly a third of them said they were not saving anything. Of those 48% said they could not afford to at this time.

—Investment Company Institute

I think two of the main reasons for the above conditions are:

1. Most people pay more than they need to for items they consume.

2. Most people pay more than they need to in taxes.

The purpose of this book is simple: to point out specific action you can take to address both these issues.

My fervent desire is that you will use the tips that are appropriate for your situation to help you achieve financial independence.

Good luck to you.

1

Give yourself a pay raise

It is easy to figure the cost of living. All you have to do is take your income and add 10 percent.

—Creative Wit

Take these actions right now to increase your income:

1. Increase your withholding allowances.

Intaxication: Euphoria at getting a refund from the IRS, which lasts until you realize that it was your money to start with.
—Washington Post word contest

Could you use an extra $132 each month? According to the Internal Revenue Service the average tax refund in 1999 was $1,589. That means that every month most workers made an interest-free loan of $132 ($1,589 ÷ by 12) to the federal government. In order to avoid doing that, increase the number of withholding allowances you are claiming. Go to www.irs.gov, click on "Individuals", click on "IRS Withholding Calculator". You will answer some questions based on your most recent pay stubs.

The calculator will estimate your tax liability for the year, and determine if you are having enough/not enough/too much money withheld from your paycheck to meet that liability.

The calculator will then recommend the number of withholding allowances you should be claiming. Armed with this information, you simply download a new W-4 from, fill it out and deliver it to your human resources office.

2. Contribute to a 401(k) plan.

This is the baseball equivalent of a "triple play". Here's why:

a. Since most employers match your contributions with at least 50 cents on the dollar up to 6 percent of your salary, you are getting a **3 percent pay raise**.

b. Since you are saving pretax dollars you are reducing your **current tax liability**.

c. The money you save earns simple and compound interest that is not taxed until you withdraw it, presumably when you are retired and in a lower tax bracket, thus reducing your **future tax liability**.

This is a fantastic deal! Yet, according to a 1999 study, 17 million eligible employees were not participating in a 401(k) Plan. Even if you cannot contribute the full amount for which you are eligible, you should contribute enough to get some of your employer's matching contribution.

Incidentally, the contribution limit was raised to $11,000 in 2002 and will gradually increase to $15,000 by 2006. If you are 50 or older, you are allowed to contribute even more through what is called a "catch up" provision. Under that provision, the amount you can contribute over and above the $11,000 increases from $1,000 in 2002 to $5,000 in 2006.

2

21 ways to cut your taxes

I am proud to be paying taxes in the United States. The only thing is - I could be just as proud for half the money.

—Arthur Godfrey

You may not be able to cut your tax bill in half, but there are definitely ways you can reduce it. Let's look at 21 of them:

1. Understand commonly used terms.

Adjusted Gross Income (AGI) — All of the income you receive during the course of the year (wages, interest, dividends, etc) minus things such as contributions to a qualified IRA, some business expenses, moving expenses and alimony payments. AGI is the first step in calculating your final tax bill.

Allowance — A number that lets your employer know how much tax to withhold from your paycheck each week in order to meet your tax obligation. This is not to be confused with an exemption. (See Exemption below)

Credits — After you figure your tax bill you can use a credit to reduce the amount of the check you have to write to the IRS. Tax credits are extremely valuable because they reduce your tax bill dollar for dollar. They are sort of like a coupon at the grocery store.

Deductions — Expenses you can subtract from your taxable income. Unlike credits, deductions do not reduce your tax bill dollar for dollar. Instead you have to use the tax table to see how much you owe. Let us say your income is $40,000 and you have deductions totaling $15,000. You would have to look at the tax table to see how much tax you owe on $25,000.

Exemption — A type of deduction that allows you to arrive at a lower taxable income. Exemptions can be claimed for yourself, your spouse and other dependents. There is a dollar amount allowed for each exemption, and this amount is subtracted from you adjusted gross income to arrive at the final amount upon which you must pay taxes.

Itemized Deductions — Expenses that can be deducted from you Adjusted Gross Income to help you arrive at a smaller income amount upon which you must calculate your tax bill. Itemized deductions include medical expenses, state/local/ property taxes, mortgage interest, charitable deductions, casualty and theft losses and miscellaneous deductions.

Progressive Taxation — The system by which higher tax rates are applied as income levels increase.

Standard Deduction — A fixed dollar amount that is determined by one's filing status, e.g. single, married filing jointly, head of household, etc. This amount eliminates the need for many taxpayers to itemize actual deductions such as medical expenses, charitable contributions or state or local taxes.

Taxable Income — Your overall income minus any allowable deductions, adjustments or exemptions. This is the final amount of income you use to determine how much tax you owe.

Withholding — Also known as pay-as-you-earn taxation, the method by which taxes are taken out of your wages as you earn them and before you receive your paycheck. The withheld taxes are placed into an IRS account and you are credited with this amount when you file your return.

2. Deduct student loan interest.

If you are paying interest on a student loan you may be able to deduct up to $2,500 in interest on your federal tax return.

For further information, see IRS Publication 970 — Tax Benefits for Education.

3. Deduct qualified medical expenses.

If your medical expenses exceed 7.5 percent of your adjusted gross income, you may be able to deduct them.

Some examples of medical expenses that you may be able to deduct are: medicine, stop-smoking programs, exercise and weight-reduction programs and travel expenses to your doctor's office or any other place at which you receive medical care.

For a complete list of deductible expenses, see IRS Publication 502 — Medical and Dental Expenses.

4. Give to charity.

There's no reason to be the richest man in the cemetery.

—Colonel Sanders

This is an opportunity to receive a tax deduction, help your favorite charity and clean out your garage and attic at the same time.

You may be able to deduct donations to charitable, religious, educational and other philanthropic organizations that have been approved by the Internal Revenue Service (IRS). In addition to donating cash, you can also give property. Make sure you get a receipt when you make your donation.

For further information, see IRS Publication 526 — Charitable Contributions.

5. Volunteer.

If you are not reimbursed for expenses you incur while doing voluntary work, you may be able to claim a charitable deduction. These expenses include things like commuting to and from the charitable organization's location, meals and lodging. You may also be able to deduct a flat mileage allowance of .14 cents per mile.

For further information, see IRS Publication 526 — Charitable Contributions.

6. Prepay your mortgage payment.

Make your January mortgage payment before December 31st and deduct the interest in the current year.

For further information, see IRS Publication 936 — Home Mortgage Interest Deduction.

7. Deduct mortgage interest.

This is potentially your largest single tax savings. For example, if you are in the 27 percent tax bracket and you pay $7,000 in interest on your mortgage you could save approximately $1,890 in federal taxes alone. This says nothing of the additional savings you would realize on your state income tax return.

For further information, see IRS Publication 936 — Home Mortgage Interest Deduction.

8. Deduct miscellaneous expenses.

If your miscellaneous expenses exceed 2% of your Adjusted Gross Income (AGI), you may be able to claim them as a deduction. Examples of miscellaneous expenses are:

o   Union dues.
o   Tax preparation fees.
o   Costs for work uniforms.
o   Expenses incurred looking for a new job.
o   Continuing education expenses.
o   Fees for safe-deposit boxes that hold investments.
o   Subscriptions to professional journals.
o   Points on your home mortgage.

This list is not all-inclusive and obviously does not apply to all taxpayers. For further information, see IRS Publication 529 — Miscellaneous Deductions.

9. Deduct "points".

If you refinanced your mortgage and paid points as a part of the loan process, you may be able to claim a tax deduction. Generally, you can deduct a percentage of the points each year over the life of the loan.

For further information, see IRS Publication 936 — Home Mortgage Interest Deduction.

10. Open a Flexible Spending Account.

Some employers offer health care spending accounts. One of the most popular is called a Flexible Spending Account (FSA). It permits you to pay for some out-of-pocket health care costs (including dental, vision and over-the-counter drugs) in pre-tax dollars. At the beginning of the year, you decide the amount you want to set aside to cover health care costs for the year.

Let us say you decide that the amount is $2400. That means that $200 would be deducted from your paycheck each month, before taxes and deposited into your Flexible Spending Account. Your spouse can do the same thing at his/her workplace. One word of caution: plan your expenses conservatively because you lose any money you deposit into your account that you do not use by the end of the year.

For further information, see IRS Publication 502 — Medical and Dental Expenses.

11. Deduct home-equity loan interest.

If you have taken out a home-equity loan you may be able to deduct up to $100,000 of interest you paid.

For further information, see IRS Publication 936 — Home Mortgage Interest Deduction.

12. Claim a first-time homebuyer credit.

To encourage home ownership, the federal government offers a tax credit to first-time homebuyers. If you fit into this category you may be eligible for such a credit.

For further information, see IRS Publication 530 — Tax Information for First Time Homebuyers.

13. Claim a child tax credit.

You may be able to claim a $1000 credit for each qualifying child below age 17.

For further information, see IRS Publication 501 — Exemptions, Standard Deductions and Filing Information.

14. Claim a child care credit.

If you hire someone to take care of your child, you may be able to claim a credit of up to $3,000 for one dependent or up to $6,000 for two or more dependents.

For more information, see IRS Publication 503 — Child and Dependent Care Expenses.

15. Claim an adoption credit.

If you adopted a child you may be eligible to claim a credit of up to $10,160 to cover the costs of the adoption.

For further information, see IRS Publication 968 — Tax Benefits for Adoption.

16. Go back to school.

If you go back to school you may be able to claim a tax deduction. The training must be either:

o   Required by your employer.
o   To maintain or improve your skills.
o   To qualify for a new trade or business.

For further information, see IRS Publication 508 — Benefits for Work-Related Education.

17. Take advantage of TRIP.

TRIP (Transportation Reimbursement Incentive Plan) allows employees to receive cash reimbursements for work-related parking and commuting expenses on a tax-free basis. You sign an election form that allows your employer to make payroll deductions equal to the cost of parking and commuting expenses. As you incur the expenses, you simply send in a request for reimbursement along with the necessary documentation. The limit is $190.00 per month for parking expenses and $100.00 per month for vanpooling or transit expenses.

Check with your Human Resources Department so see if your company offers TRIP.

18. File your tax return as "Head of household."

Since your filing status helps determine how much you pay in taxes, use the most advantageous filing status you are allowed. If you are single but maintain a household for over half the year for a child, grandchild or other dependent relative, you may be able to file your return as Head of Household, which has a lower tax rate than filing as a single person.

For further information, see IRS Publication 17 — Your Federal Income Tax.

19. Start a home-based business.

Every North American taxpayer who works a full time job and does not have a side business is probably overpaying taxes to the tune of between $3,000 and $9,000 every year.

—Sandy Botkin, Former IRS Tax Attorney

With a home-based business you get to use a portion of your home for business and claim tax deductions for expenses that you would have anyway. Some examples are insurance, utilities, repairs, and the cost for installing a security system. You can also depreciate a part of your home as a business asset.

To get further information, see IRS Publications 587 — Business Use of Home.

20. Hire your kids.

If you are a sole proprietor or have a husband and wife partnership you may be able to hire your kids if they are under age 18. The advantages are:

o   You may be able to claim a business tax deduction for their salary (which is money you probably would have given them anyway).

o   Since they are under 18, you may avoid the employer share of FICA on their salary.

For further information, see IRS Publication 535 — Business Expenses.

21. Deduct health insurance premiums.

If you are self-employed, you may be able to deduct 100 percent of your health insurance premium.

For further information, see IRS Publication 535 — Business Expenses.

3

Cut your grocery bill in half

With the typical family spending approximately $2,700 per year on groceries, it is no wonder that someone said, "The most expensive vehicle to operate, per mile, is the grocery cart."

However, you can drastically cut your expenses without sacrificing nutrition.

Before going to the store:

1. Take inventory of what you have on hand.

In addition to preventing you from purchasing things you already have, it helps with meal planning.

2. Decide how much you are going to spend.

It might be helpful to set a price per person per meal goal. For example: Breakfast =1$ person, Dinner $4 person.

3. Plan your menus based on what's on sale.

4. Make your grocery list based on planned menus.

Some estimates show that people who shop without a list spend as much as 40% more than they do when they have a list.

5. Eat something.

This will help you avoid impulse purchases. By the way, studies show that people spend about 10% more when they shop on an empty stomach.

6. Buy several copies of the Sunday paper.

You will be able to collect more coupons so you can stock up on products you use regularly. The savings will more than offset the cost of the newspapers.

7. Get coupons from the Internet.

There are two big advantages to getting coupons on the web: higher value and longer expiration dates. Some of the best internet coupon sites are: **www.valuepage.com**, **www. coupons.com**, **www.couponcart.com**, **www.cutthehunger. com**, **www.eversave.com**, **www.goodhousekeeping.com**, **www.coolsavings.com**, **www.smartsource.com**, **www. thefrugalshopper.com**.

8. Go directly to the source.

Get coupons from manufacturers by calling their 800 number. You will be amazed at how willing they are to send you coupons. If you do not have their number call long distance directory assistance (1-800-555-1212) and get it. You can also get coupons by going to their website.

9. Organize your coupons.

In order to not forget coupons or miss expiration dates, take some envelopes and label them according to the items you normally purchase, e.g. frozen vegetables, cereal, canned goods, etc. When you clip coupons place them into the appropriate envelopes.
Use the envelopes when making up your shopping list. **www. cutthehunger.com** will show you how to organize your coupons in ten minutes.

10. Look for stores that double or triple coupons.

11. Forget loyalty to a particular store.

Shop where you can get the best "Bang for your Buck". This may mean having one store where you buy bulk nonperishable items and another store where you buy regular items.

12. Be sure to take your coupons to the store.

I am still amazed at the number of people who forget and leave their coupons on the kitchen table. I always paperclip mine to the shopping list.

13. Plan to shop alone during non-peak hours.

It's important to compare price-per-ounce, or other unit prices on shelf labels. If pressed for time or distracted by little helpers, you may not be able to do comparisons. Monday and Tuesday are usually the least busy days.

14. Read coupons carefully.

This helps you avoid checkout surprises. Highlight "Good on any", or "Good on only" and "Expiration date".

15. Change what you shop for.

If you do not see coupons for brands that you regularly use, consider changing to brands for which you do see coupons.

At the store:

1. Buy nonperishable items in bulk.

Purchase items like canned goods, sugar, and flour in bulk when they are on sale.

2. Buy cheese in bulk and shred it yourself.

3. Use one coupon for each item purchased, even if you purchase more than one of the item.

Coupons generally say one coupon per purchase. But, if you have three coupons and purchase three cans of soup, for example, that's three purchases.

4. Make friends with the department heads.

They can tell you about any special deals and markdowns that are available or will be coming up soon.

5. Use a price book.

You will want to recognize a true bargain and to be able to buy in bulk when the price goes down. You can use a three ring binder. Make several columns on the page: Date, Store, Item, Unit Price, and Total price. At the top of the page put the name of the items you normally buy such as bread, cereal, cheese, milk, etc. As you are shopping, you can write down the prices. In the future, this becomes the reference point for determining if something is a real bargain.

6. Buy items that are approaching their expiration date.

They are usually significantly discounted. For example, I recently bought porterhouse steak for $3.34 per pound. The regular price had been $9.49 per pound, but they were on sale and they were approaching their expiration date. Either cook the meat the day you purchase it or freeze it.

7. Buy store brands.

You can save as much as 30 – 40%. By the way, the same manufacturers who make the more – expensive name brand products make many store brands.

8. Never buy toiletries at the grocery store.

If you purchase items like toothpaste, mouthwash, and contact lens solution you could pay from 30 to 90 percent more than you would if you purchased those items at a discount drug store or Target or Wal-Mart.

9. Look "low".

Since manufacturers pay premium dollars to get their products placed at eye level, that is where the highest priced items are. Get lower prices by selecting the same product but only getting it off the bottom shelf.

10. Don't buy things that you think your family should eat but they never do.

If you buy cauliflower every week for $2 with the intention of eating more healthily but it winds up going bad, you could save $100 per year simply by not buying any more cauliflower.

11. Join the supermarket's savings club.

This gets you their newsletter, 5% off coupons, and other "member only" specials.

12. Stockpile staples.

You don't want to run out of something and have to pay the full price. Pasta, dried fruit, rice and beans are great because they last.

13. Request price matching.

Look for stores that will honor all competitors' ads. By not driving all over town to get the best price, you save money, gas and time.

14. Take a rain check.

If your store is offering a great price on a product that you normally use, but they are out of stock, ask for a rain check.

15. Look for holiday freebies.

Some supermarkets will give you a free (or reduced price) ham or turkey if you spend a certain amount of money.

16. Stock up after Thanksgiving.

Since there are more coupons issued during November and December than any other months, these are great times to combine coupon savings with pre- and post holiday sales.

17. Check the weight before putting it in the cart.

Sometimes a 5-pound bag of onions or potatoes is really 4 pounds.

18. Watch for checkout mistakes.

Scanners make mistakes – usually on items that are on sale. Watch the monitor during checkout to make sure you are getting the sale price. Also, since there is no bar code on a head of cabbage or lettuce, the cashier will sometimes mistakenly charge by the pound rather than by the head.

19. Buy less meat.

About 30% of the typical food budget goes for meat.

20. Plan to use your freezer.

Buy things like ground beef and chicken breasts in bulk and separate it into smaller servings and freeze it. Freeze soups and stews.

21. Keep a running total as you shop.

This helps you stay within the amount you have planned to spend.

22. Shop with cash.

This also helps you stay within the amount you have planned to spend, since you are handing over "real" money, unlike if you use a check or a credit card.

23. Combine savings.

The ideal situation is to purchase an item that is on sale, is approaching its expiration date, you have a manufacturer coupon, a store coupon and a manufacturer rebate. If you can't reach the ideal, get as close as possible.

24. Hand your coupons to the cashier in advance.

That way you don't forget to use them.

25. Get in and get out.

Studies show that after 30 minutes, people spend approximately $.50 more for every minute they remain in the store.

At home:

1. Check your receipt for errors.

2. Make your drinks.

Buy powdered mix and make your own soft drinks. For an extra treat, use fresh fruit, yogurt and ice cubes to make a smoothie.

3. Limit kids portions.

Parents often give kids an adult-sized portion and wind up either eating it themselves (at the expense of their waistline) or throwing it out. Give kids a smaller portion and if they are still hungry give them some more.

4. Look for manufacturer's rebates.

Look carefully as sometimes they are on the back of or even inside the box.

5. Make it yourself.

With our on-the-go lives we can slip into convenience. Be aware that there is a huge cost for this.

For example, on a recent trip to the supermarket I noticed these differences:

Convenience	Make it yourself
Peeled carrots = $1.65/lb.	Unpeeled carrots = 0.99/lb.
Sliced turkey =$6.99/lb.	Whole turkey =$ 0.49/lb.
Sliced ham = $5.99/lb.	Whole ham = $2.39/lb.

6. Use leftovers.

Tonight's baked chicken can easily become tomorrow night's chicken salad. This helps avoid throwing away food. According to studies, the average family throws away between 15 – 25% of the food they purchase. This comes to almost $700 per year.

7. Cook in advance.

In her book, "Frozen Assets: How to Cook for a Day and Eat for a Month", Deborah Taylor-Hough says she cut her monthly food bill for her family of five from $700 to $300. She did it by cooking a month's worth of food ahead of time and freezing it in family-size portions.

You may not be willing to cook a month's worth of food, but you can cook on Sunday for the entire week and freeze it in dinner-size containers. Stews, soup and chili are particularly suited for this approach.

8. Have a soup and bread night.

You save on meat and the family has a good nutritious meal. We recently had a tomato soup along with some crusty bread and it was delicious.

9. Buy produce at a farmer's market.

You save money because there is no middleman involved as there is with the supermarket. You can save even more by going late in the day. The farmers obviously don't want to pack up and carry the stuff away. Visit **www.localharvest.org** to find farmer's markets in your area.

10. Use frozen fruit juice cubes to add flavor to water.

This saves on soda. You can make the cubes by freezing juice from natural or canned fruit in ice cube trays.

11. Make your own party trays.

You will save a lot of money compared to having the store create them for you.

4

Wipe out $1800 in credit card debt

1. Understand commonly used credit card terms:

Annual percentage rate (APR) — A yearly rate of interest that includes fees and costs paid to acquire the loan. Lenders are required by law to disclose the APR. The rate is calculated in a standard way, taking the average compound interest rate over the term of the loan, so borrowers can compare loans.

Average daily balance — This is the method by which most credit card issuers calculate the amount of your payment that is due. An average daily balance is determined by adding each day's balance and dividing the total by the number of days in the billing cycle. The average daily balance is then multiplied by the card's monthly periodic rate, which is calculated by dividing the annual percentage rate by 12. A card with an annual percentage rate of 18 percent would have a monthly periodic rate of 1.5 percent.

Balance transfer — The process of moving an unpaid credit card debt from one issuer to another. Card issuers sometimes offer teaser rates to encourage balance transfers coming in and balance-transfer fees to discourage them from going out.

Cash-advance fee — A charge by the bank for using credit cards to obtain cash. This fee can be stated in terms of a flat per-transaction fee or a percentage of the amount of the cash advance. For example, the fee may be expressed as follows: "2%/$10". This means that the cash advance fee will be the greater of 2 percent of the cash advance amount or $10. Depending on the bank issuing the card, the cash advance fee may be deducted directly from the cash advance at the time the money is received or it may be posted to your bill as of the day you received the advance. The cost of a cash advance is also higher because there generally is no grace period. Interest accrues from the moment the money is withdrawn.

Cardholder agreement — The written statement that gives the terms and conditions of a credit card account. The cardholder agreement is required by Federal Reserve regulations. It must include the Annual Percentage Rate, the monthly minimum payment formula, annual fee if applicable, and the cardholder's rights in billing disputes.

Changes in the cardholder agreement may be made, with written advance notice, at any time by the issuer. Rules for imposing changes vary from state to state, but the rules that apply are those of the home state of the issuing bank, not the home state of the cardholder.

Finance charge — The charge for using a credit card, comprised of interest costs and other fees.

Floor — The minimum rate possible on a variable-rate loan or line of credit, after any initial introductory rate period. For example, on a credit card with the Prime rate as its index, no matter how low the Prime rate drops, the rate on the line may never decrease below the stated rate floor.

Grace period — If the credit card user does not carry a balance, the grace period is the interest-free time a lender allows between the transaction date and the billing date. The standard grace period is usually between 20 and 30 days. If there is no grace period, finance charges will accrue the moment a purchase is made with the credit card. People who carry a balance on their credit cards have no grace period.

Minimum payment — The minimum amount a cardholder can pay to keep the account from going into default. Some card issuers will set a high minimum if they are uncertain of the cardholder's ability to pay. Most card issuers require a minimum payment of two percent of the outstanding balance.

Over-the-limit fee — A fee charged for exceeding the credit limit on the card.

Periodic rate — The interest rate described in relation to a specific amount of time. The monthly periodic rate, for example, is the cost of credit per month; the daily periodic rate is the cost of credit per day.

Pre-approved — A credit card offer with "pre-approved" only means that a potential customer has passed a preliminary credit-information screening. A credit card company can spurn the customers it invited with "pre-approved" junk mail if it doesn't like the applicant's credit rating.

Secured card — A credit card that a cardholder secures with a savings deposit to ensure payment of the outstanding balance if the cardholder defaults on payments. It is used by people new to credit, or people trying to rebuild their poor credit ratings.

Teaser rate — Often called the introductory rate, it is the below-market interest rate offered to entice customers to switch credit cards or lenders.

Variable interest rate — Percentage that a borrower pays for the use of money, and which moves up or down periodically based on changes in other interest rates.

2. Decide when you want to be debt-free.

Go to **www.bankrate.com/dls/calc/credcardpay.asp**
Enter the desired months until you are debt-free.
Enter your credit card balance.
Enter the interest rate.

It will tell you how long it will take you to pay off your credit card. You can also play "What If" by lowering the interest rate and see what impact that has on the time it will take you to pay off the balance.

3. Use one "charge" card.

This should be a card with a "cash back" feature such as the Discover Card that gives a rebate if you use the card to charge purchases during a given month. Use the card for things for which you would otherwise pay cash or write a check, e.g. groceries, gas, etc. Since the goal is to never pay interest or a late fee, pay the full amount when you receive the statement. By doing that, you are actually using the card to make money.

4. Take advantage of the grace period on your "charge card".

Suppose your credit card period starts on the first on the month and on the first you buy $150 worth of groceries and pay with your Discover card. You get to keep the $150 in your interest-bearing account until the statement arrives – maybe as long as 45 days after you made the purchase.

5. Stop using the card(s) that you want to pay off.

Trying to pay off a credit card while continuing to use it is like fighting a war to achieve peace. You can't get there from here.

6. Negotiate a lower APR.

Most card issuers are willing to give you a lower rate, particularly if you tell them you have a lower offer from another company. A lower APR obviously means that more of your payment goes to reduce the principle.

7. Ask the card issuer to waive the annual fee.

There is no reason to pay an annual fee for the privilege of paying an average APR of 14%.

8. Take advantage of an introductory APR of 0%.

This is a great way to apply more of your payment to the principle on the card you are paying off. You simply accept the new card and transfer your balance to it. During the introductory period (usually 6 months) every dollar you pay goes to reduce the balance.

Here are some words of caution:

o   Make sure there is no balance transfer fee, because it could eat up your savings.

o   Make sure you know what the APR will be at the end of the introductory period.

o   Make your payments on time or the APR could increase astronomically.

9. Make a payment every two weeks.

Interest on an unpaid balance accumulates daily. Because federal law requires credit card issuers to apply payments the day they arrive, the sooner you get your payment in, the less interest you pay. In effect you are using the credit card issuer's strategy (daily interest) against them.

Here's how it works: Let's say your minimum payment is $200 and is due on the 27th of the month. You can make a payment of $100 on the first and a payment of $100 on the 15th. If you keep doing that, you will see the balance drop dramatically.

10. Pay more than the minimum.

Let us say that you have a credit card balance of $3,000 with an annual percentage rate (APR) of 18 percent.

The minimum monthly payment is 2% of the unpaid balance = $60.

By paying $60 per month, at the end of 8 years when the balance is paid in full you will have paid $5,780. Remember, the original balance was $3,000.

If you pay $110 each month:

You will pay off the balance in 3 years.

The total payments would equal $3,980, which is a savings of **$1,800** ($5780 - $3980).

11. Pay on time.

The average late fee more than doubled between 1992 and 2000, from $12.53 to $27.61. In addition to the late fee, many credit card issuers will raise the interest rate on your card if you are late. Plan on mailing your payment a 7 to 10 days before it is due.

12. Read your statement every month.

A recent study showed that 26% of Americans ages 35 to 44 are not aware of their card's interest rate, and 17% fail to review their monthly card statements.

As Pete Seeger said, "Education is what you get when you read the fine print. Experience is what you get when you don't." So read the fine print.

5

Eliminate over $60,000 from your mortgage

This house has every convenience except low monthly payments.
— New homeowner

With a little bit of strategy you can easily eliminate several mortgage payments and save thousands of dollars in the process.

Assume that you have a fixed-rate $220,000 mortgage @7.25% for 30 years that you took out on January 16, 2004. The monthly payment is $1500.79 per month.

The pay-off date would be January 16, 2034.

The total payments would be **$320,283.61**

If you add $100 to your payment -

The pay-off date would be August 16, 2028, 6 years early.

The total payments would be **$251,413.39**

Total savings: $68,870.22

To see how much you can save on your mortgage:

o   Go to **www.howstuffworks.com**

o   Click on "Mortgages".

o   Click on "How mortgages work".

o   Go to "Table of Contents".

o   Click on "Ways to save money".

o   Click on "Make extra payments".

o   Click on "This calculator".

6

Slash your utility costs

Based on the national average, the typical household's utility costs break down as follows:

44% heating and cooling
33% lighting, cooking and other appliances
14% water heating
 9% refrigerator

There are a number of ways to reduce your expenditures in each of these areas:

A. Cut lighting cost by 50%.

According to the Department of Energy, if you replace 25% of your lights in high-use areas (kitchen, den, hallways) with mini fluorescent bulbs, you can cut up to 50% off your lighting bill. The specific benefits of mini fluorescent bulbs over incandescent ones are:

o   They use ¼ the energy.
o   They last up to 10 times longer.
o   They produce more light per watt.
o   They give off 90% less heat.

www.energystar.gov/stores/storelocator.asp has a listing of mini fluorescent bulb dealers.

B. Cut heating costs by 10%.

1. Install a programmable thermostat.

According to the Department of Energy, you can save as much as 10% a year on your heating bill by simply turning your thermostat back 10% to 15% for 8 hours. You can do this automatically without sacrificing comfort by installing a programmable thermostat. This allows you to adjust the temperature according to a pre-set schedule. As a result, the heating or cooling system does not kick in as much when you are asleep or when the house is not occupied. Programmable thermostats can store and repeat multiple daily settings (six or more temperature settings a day). You have the added flexibility of being able to manually override a setting without affecting the rest of the daily or weekly program.

Be aware that these thermostats do not work with heat pumps.

2. Set your thermostat as low as is comfortable.

According to the Department of Energy, for every degree you lower the thermostat setting, you can save up to 3% on your heating bill. So you may want to set your thermostat at 68° in the winter.

3. Install new storm windows.

According to the Department of Energy, this can reduce heat loss by as much as 25 – 50%.

4. Weatherize your storm windows.

This can serve as a less expensive alternative to replacing windows.

5. Limit use of exhausts fans.

In just one hour, these fans can send a houseful of warmed air outdoors. Turn the fan off as soon as it has done its job.

6. Use drapes.

Close your curtains and shades at night; open them during the day. This allows the sun to help with heating your house.

7. Keep windows on the south side of your house clean.

This also allows the sun to help with heating your house.

8. Caulk and seal air leaks.

This applies to places where plumbing, ductwork, or electrical wiring penetrates through exterior walls, floors and ceilings.

9. Install rubber gaskets where needed.

Outlet and switch plates on exterior walls are sources for losing heat. By installing rubber gaskets you eliminate significant sources of heat loss.

10. Clean or replace furnace filters monthly or as needed.

Clogged or dirty filters cause your system to work less efficiently, thus increasing your heating costs.

11. Close off unused room.

Close an unoccupied room that is isolated from the rest of the house, and turn down the thermostat or turn off the heat for that room or zone. However, do not turn the heating off if it adversely affects the rest of your system.

For example, if you use a heat pump, do not close the vents because that could damage the heat pump.

12. Consider a heat pump.

If you use electricity to heat your home, consider installing an energy-efficient heat pump system. It can trim the amount of electricity you use for heating by as much as 30% to 40%.

13. Protect your thermostat from cold air drafts.

By doing so your heating system turns on only when you need extra warmth.

14. Schedule an annual check-up for your heating system.

By scheduling an annual check-up, you not only insure that the system is working efficiently, but you also extend its life.

15. Set your thermostat back to 55° if you will be gone for a few days.

This is warm enough to keep the pipes from freezing but will save you money because the furnace will not come on much. Note: If you have a heat pump, do not set your thermostat back during heating season. Just find a comfortable setting and leave it there. Lowering the setting on a heat pump system will cause the backup heat to come on when it's raised in the morning. Backup heat uses a lot more energy than the normal heat mode, meaning you'll waste more energy than you may have saved during the night.

16. Seal the chimney.

This helps you save if you never use your fireplace.

17. Keep your fireplace damper closed unless a fire is going.

Keeping the damper open is like keeping a 48-inch window wide open during the winter. It allows warm air to go right up the chimney.

18. When you use the fireplace, lower the thermostat setting to between 50° and 55°.

19. Install tempered glass doors and a heat-air exchange system on your fireplace.

This blows warmed air back into the room.

20. Make the flue damper seal as snug as possible.

21. Caulk around the fireplace hearth.

22. Use grates made of c-shaped metal tubes.

They draw cool room air into the fireplace and circulate warm air back into the room.

23. Clear warm-air registers, baseboard heaters, and radiators.

Make sure they're not blocked by furniture, carpeting, or drapes.

C. Cut cooling cost by $250 per year.

1. Plant trees.

The most effective way to keep your home cool is to prevent the heat from building up in the first place. A primary source of heat buildup is sunlight absorbed by your home's roof, walls, and windows. The solution: Plant trees or shrubs to shade the air-conditioning unit(s). According to the Department of Energy, just three trees, properly placed around the house, can save an average household between $100 and $250 in cooling energy costs annually.

2. Install a programmable thermostat.

According to the Department of Energy, you can save as much as 10% a year on your cooling bill by simply turning your thermostat back 10% to 15% for 8 hours. You can do this automatically without sacrificing comfort by installing a programmable thermostat. This allows you to adjust the temperature according to a pre-set schedule.

As a result, you don't operate the equipment as much when you are asleep or when the house or part of the house is not occupied. Programmable thermostats can store and repeat multiple daily settings (six or more temperature settings a day). You have added flexibility in that you can manually override one setting without affecting the rest of the daily or weekly program.

3. Set your thermostat as high as you can comfortably stand it.

The less difference between the indoor and outdoor temperatures, the lower your overall cooling bill will be. Try keeping the thermostat set at 78°. According to the Department of Energy, for every degree you raise the thermostat setting, you can save up to 3% on your cooling bill.

4. Clean or replace furnace filters once a month or as needed.

5. Clear warm-air registers, baseboard heaters, and radiators.

Make sure they're not blocked by furniture, carpeting, or drapes. A dirty or clogged filter reduces the efficiency of your system and increases cooling costs.

6. Limit the use of exhaust fans.

In just one hour, these fans can send a houseful of cooled air outdoors. Turn the fan off as soon as it has done its job.

7. Use draperies.

Keep the draperies and shades on your south facing windows closed during the day to prevent sunlight from entering your home.

8. Close off unused room.

Close an unoccupied room that is isolated from the rest of the house, and turn up the thermostat or turn off the cooling for that room or zone.

9. Remove grass, weeds and leaves from around the outdoor unit of your cooling system.

When airflow is blocked, it puts a strain on the system, lowers efficiency and increases cooling costs.

10. Shade room air conditioners from direct sunlight.

This reduces their workload and lowers cooling costs.

11. Raise the thermostat setting when you go out.

12. Install white shades, drapes or blinds.

This will reflect hot sunlight away from the house.

13. Set the thermostat fan to shut off at the same time as the compressor.

In other words, don't use the system's central fan to circulate air. Instead, use fans in individual rooms.

14. Do summer cooking in the evening.

That way your home stays more comfortable during the day.

15. Use a whole-house fan.

Whole-house fans help cool your home by pulling cool air through the house and exhausting warm air through the attic. They are effective when operated at night and when the outside air is cooler than the inside air.

16. Use an interior fan in conjunction with your window air conditioner.

This spreads the cooled air more effectively through your home without greatly increasing your power use.

17. Don't place lamps or TV sets near your air-conditioning thermostat.

The thermostat senses heat from these appliances, which can cause the compressor to run longer than necessary.

18. Apply a reflective coating to your roof.

Dull and dark-colored house exteriors absorb 70 to 90 percent of the sun's energy. Light-colored surfaces, on the other hand, reflect most of the heat away from your house.

19. Schedule an annual check-up for your cooling system.

By keeping your system in optimal working condition, you'll not only reduce energy costs, but also extend your system's service life.

D. Cut cooking cost.

1. Don't open the oven door to check on food any more than necessary.

Twenty-five percent of the heat escapes each time you do.

2. Turn off the oven about 15 to 20 minutes before the end of the cooking time.

The leftover heat will finish the job.

3. Cook in oven-safe glass or ceramic pans.

They allow you to set your oven temperature twenty-five degrees lower than the recipe calls for.

4. Keep pots and pans covered and use the right size pot or pan for the size of your stove's burner.

5. Use properly fitted lids to hold the heat in.

6. When boiling a liquid, only put the amount into the pot that you need.

7. Begin a self-cleaning cycle while your oven is still hot from cooking.

8. Cook several dishes in the oven at the same time.

9. Partially thaw frozen foods in the refrigerator before cooking them.

In many cases, thawing foods cuts the cooking time by a third.

E. Cut dishwasher cost.

Studies show electric dishwashers use less hot water than washing and rinsing dishes by hand.

1. When you purchase a dishwasher, look for one with a short or light cycle.

They require fewer fills and less hot water.

2. Only run full loads.

3. Check the condition of your dishwasher filter screen and clean or replace it when necessary.

F. Cut the cost of washing clothes.

1. Wash full loads only.

2. Use the maximum washing time only for heavily soiled clothes.

Washing longer than necessary wastes energy and wears out clothes.

3. Vary the size of garments in a load so water can circulate freely.

4. Use warm or cold water for washing and always use cold water to rinse.

G. Cut the cost of drying clothes.

1. During the summer, run the dryer at night so its warmth isn't released during the heat of the day.

2. Clear the lint screen after each load for quick drying.

3. Use the moisture control features.

Drying more than needed wastes energy and wears out clothes.

4. Check the outside vent lid monthly to make sure it is not clogged.

If it doesn't close tightly, replace it with one that does to keep outside air from leaking into the house.

5. Never overload your dryer.

6. Dry loads of clothing back to back, using the leftover heat.

This reduces overall drying time and lowers energy costs.

H. Cut refrigerator and freezer cost.

1. Don't place your refrigerator next to your stove or other sources of heat.

Giving a refrigerator or freezer "room to breath" lets it operate more efficiently and prevents premature burnout.

2. Store the most perishable items in the coldest part of your refrigerator (usually the back or top shelf).

This allows you to set the temperature slightly higher.

3. Vacuum the coils.

Dirt and dust on the coils greatly reduce efficiency. Move your refrigerator out from the wall and vacuum its condenser coils once a year. Your refrigerator will run for shorter periods with clean coils.

4. Allow hot foods to cool before putting them into the refrigerator.

Hot foods make the refrigerator run for longer periods.

5. Cover food before placing it into the refrigerator.

Uncovered foods release moisture and make the compressor work harder.

6. Be sure your refrigerator door closes tightly.

Conduct a test by closing the door over a piece of paper or a dollar bill so it is half in and half out of the refrigerator. If you can pull the paper or bill out easily, you may need to adjust the latch or replace the seal.

7. Don't keep your refrigerator or freezer too cold.

Recommended temperatures are 37° to 40°F for the fresh food compartment of the refrigerator and 5°F for the freezer section. If you have a separate freezer for long-term storage, you should keep it at 0°F. To check refrigerator temperature, place an appliance thermometer in a glass of water in the center of the refrigerator. Read it after 24 hours. To check the freezer temperature, place a thermometer between frozen packages. Read it after 24 hours.

8. Regularly defrost manual-defrost refrigerators and freezers.

Frost buildup increases the amount of energy needed to keep the motor running. Don't allow frost to build up more than one-quarter of an inch.

I. Cut water heating cost.

1. Repair leaky faucets promptly.

A leak of one drop per second wastes more than 250 gallons of water a month, plus the energy used to heat it.

2. Insulate your electric hot-water storage tank and pipes.

3. Install aerating low-flow faucets and showerheads.

This can reduce water use by 50-70 percent.

4. Lower the thermostat on your water heater.

Water heaters sometimes come from the factory with high temperature settings, but a setting of 115°F provides comfortable hot water for most uses.

5. Drain a quart of water from your water tank every 3 months.

This removes sediment that impedes heat transfer and lowers the efficiency of your heater. The type of water tank you have determines the steps to take, so follow the manufacturer's advice.

6. Take more showers than baths.

Bathing uses the most hot water in the average household. You use 15-25 gallons of hot water for a bath, but less than 10 gallons during a 5-minute shower.

J. Cut the cost of flushing toilets by 50%.

Purchase a water-saving replacement toilet.

Comparison of average water costs

	Typical existing unit	New unit
Gallons per flush (gpf)	3.5	1.6
Annual gallons used	27,300	12,500
Annual Water Cost	$110	$50
Lifetime Water Cost	$880	$400

K. Reduce your telephone bill.

1. Disconnect non-essential options.

You can probably live without such options as 3-way calling, call waiting, voice mail and caller ID. Someone said we have voice mail to screen calls, and then we have call waiting so we won't miss a call from someone that we probably did not want to talk to anyway.

2. Use dial-up for Internet service instead of the faster-connecting DSL or cable connection.

DSL or cable costs $40 - $60 per month while the dial-up lines cost $12-25.

3. Get free Internet access from Netzero.

Visit them at **www.netzero.com**

4. Avoid using directory assistance.

This could cost 30 cents for a local number and up to $2 for a long distance number. Use the telephone directory or the free Internet directory assistance.

5. Make sure your cell phone plan matches your calling patterns.

Since cell phone companies have added an extra hour to peak time, if you are still accumulating extra charges, contact your carrier and switch to another plan.

6. Shop for the lowest long distance providers.

Compare rates for the five largest long distance carriers at **www. trac.org**.

7. Go for one-rate service.

Some of the larger companies such as MCI, Sprint and AT&T now have a plan in which they charge a flat rate for local service and unlimited long distance service. The monthly charge is $49.00.

7

Increase your gas mileage by 33%

The high cost of gasoline doesn't have to bust your budget.

—American Automobile Association and
Federal Trade Commission

Applying these tips will enable you to save lots of money as you drive:

1. Avoid aggressive driving.

According to the Environmental Protection Agency, aggressive driving (speeding, rapid acceleration and braking) lowers gas mileage by up to 33 percent on the road and by 5 percent around town.

2. Follow the speed limit.

Gas mileage decreases rapidly at speeds above 60 mph. Each 5 mph you drive over 60 mph is like paying an additional $0.10 per gallon for gas. Observing the speed limit is also safer.

3. Replace the oxygen sensor.

Replacing a faulty oxygen sensor may improve your gas mileage by as much as 40 percent.

4. Remove the roof racks.

A loaded roof rack can decrease your fuel economy by 5 percent.

5. Replace the air filter.

Replacing a clogged air filter not only improves your car's gas mileage by as much as 10 percent, but protects your engine as well.

6. Keep tires properly inflated.

You can improve your gas mileage by aproximately 3.3 percent by keeping your tires inflated to the proper pressure. Properly inflated tires are also safer and last longer.

7. Avoid carrying unneeded items.

An extra 100 lbs in the trunk reduces a typical car's fuel economy by 1-2 percent.

8. Keep your engine properly tuned.

This can improve gas mileage by 4 percent.

9. Combine errands.

Several short trips taken from a cold start can use twice as much fuel as a longer multipurpose trip covering the same distance when the engine is warm. Trip planning ensures that traveling is done when the engine is warmed-up and efficient.

8

15 ways to cut your health insurance cost

I thought my group health insurance plan was fine until I found out I couldn't collect unless the whole group is sick.

—Bob Phillips

1. Understand commonly used health insurance terms:

Ancillary Services — Services, other than those provided by a physician or hospital, which are related to a patient's care, such as laboratory work, x-rays and anesthesia.

Calendar Year — The period beginning January 1 of any year through December 31 of the same year.

Case Management — A process whereby a covered person with specific health care needs has his/her care coordinated among various heath care providers.

Certificate of Coverage — A document given to an insured that describes the benefits, limitations and exclusions of coverage provided by an insurance company.

Claim — Information a medical provider or insured submits to an insurance company to request payment for medical services provided to the insured.

Coinsurance — The portion of covered health care costs for which the covered person has a financial responsibility, usually a fixed percentage. Coinsurance usually applies after the insured meets his/her deductible.

Consolidated Omnibus Budget Reconciliation Act (COBRA) — A federal law that, among other things, requires employers to offer continued health insurance coverage to certain employees and their beneficiaries whose group health insurance has been terminated if they undergo a triggering event.

Contract Year — The period of time from the effective date of the contract to the expiration date of the contract.

Coordination of Benefits (COB) — A provision in the contract that applies when a person is covered under more than one medical plan. It requires that payment of benefits be coordinated by all plans to eliminate over-insurance or duplication of benefits.

Co-payment — A cost-sharing arrangement in which an insured pays a specified charge for a specified service, such as $10 for an office visit. The insured is usually responsible for payment at the time the service is rendered. This charge may be in addition to certain coinsurance and deductible payments.

Covered Person — An individual who meets eligibility requirements and for whom premium payments are paid for specified benefits of the contractual agreement.

Deductible — The amount of eligible expenses a covered person must pay each year from his/her own pocket before the plan will make payment for eligible benefits.

Deductible Carry Over Credit — Charges applied to the deductible for services during the last 3 months of a calendar year that may be used to satisfy the following year's deductible.

Dependent — A covered person who relies on another person for support or obtains health coverage through a spouse, parent or grandparent who is the covered person under a plan.

Effective Date — The date insurance coverage begins.

Eligible Dependent — A dependent of a covered person (spouse, child, or other dependent) who meets all requirements specified in the contract to qualify for coverage and for whom premium payment is made.

Eligible Expenses — The lower of the reasonable and customary charges or the agreed upon health services fee for health services and supplies covered under a health plan.

Explanation of Benefits (EOB) — The statement send to an insured by their health insurance company listing services provided, amount billed, eligible expenses and payment made by the health insurance company.

Insured — A person who has obtained health insurance coverage under a health insurance plan.

Managed Care — A health care system under which physicians, hospitals, and other health care professionals are organized into a group or "network" in order to manage the cost, quality and access to health care. Managed care organizations include Preferred Provider Organizations (PPOs) and Health Maintenance Organizations (HMOs).

Out-of-Pocket Maximum — The total payments that must be paid by a covered person (i.e., deductibles and coinsurance) as defined by the contract. Once this limit is reached, covered health services are paid at 100% for health services received during the rest of that calendar year.

Participating Provider — A medical provider who has been contracted to render medical services or supplies to policyholder at a pre-negotiated fee. Providers include hospitals, physicians, and other medical facilities.

Preferred Provider Organization (PPO) — A health care delivery arrangement which offers policyholders access to participating providers at reduced costs. PPOs provide insured's incentives, such as lower deductibles and co-payments, to use providers in the network. Network providers agree to negotiate fees in exchange for their preferred provider status.

Provider — A physician, hospital, health professional and other entity or institutional health care provider that provides a health care service.

Primary Care Physician (PCP) — A physician that is responsible for providing, prescribing, authorizing and coordinating all medical care and treatment.

Reasonable and Customary (R &C) — A term used to refer to the commonly charged or prevailing fees for health services within a geographic area. A fee is generally considered to be reasonable if it falls within the parameters of the average or commonly charged fee for the particular service within that specific community.

Underwriting — The act of reviewing and evaluating prospective policyholder for risk assessment and appropriate premium.

2. Analyze your needs.

Think about your personal situation. After all, you may not mind that pregnancy is not covered, but you may want coverage for psychological counseling. You also do not want to pay the higher premium for a PPO if an HMO will meet your needs. Do you want coverage for your whole family or just yourself? Are you concerned with preventive care and checkups? Would you be comfortable in a managed care setting that might restrict your choices somewhat but give you broad coverage and convenience? These are questions that only you can answer.

3. Shop around for the best premium.

Premiums can vary by as much as 50% for the same person. So, once you have determined the type of plan that meets your needs, shop around for the best premium. Whether you end up choosing a fee-for-service plan or a form of managed care, you must examine a benefits summary or an outline of coverage—the description of policy benefits, exclusions, and provisions that make it easier to understand a particular policy and compare it with others.

You can use the attached checklist to compare premiums and coverage:

Health Insurance Checklist

Place a check next to covered medical services

Inpatient hospital services
Outpatient surgery
Physician visits (in the hospital)
Office visits
Skilled nursing care
Medical tests and X-rays
Prescription drugs
Mental health care
Drug and alcohol abuse treatment
Home health care visits
Rehabilitation facility care
Physical therapy
Speech therapy
Hospice care
Maternity care
Chiropractic treatment
Preventive care and checkups
Well-baby care
Dental care
Other covered services
Are there any medical service limits, exclusions, or preexisting conditions that will affect you or your family?

What types of utilization review, preauthorization, or certification procedures are included?

How much is the premium?
$

[ ] month   [ ] quarter   [ ] year

Are there any discounts available for good health or healthy behaviors (e.g., non-smoker)?

_____

How much is the annual deductible?

$_____ per person

$_____ per family

What coinsurance or co-payments apply?

_____% after I meet my deductible

$_____co-pay or % coinsurance per office visit

$_____co-pay or % coinsurance for "wellness" care (includes well-baby care, annual eye exam, physical, etc.)

$_____% co-pay or coinsurance for inpatient hospital care

4. Raise your deductible.

This can lower your premium by as much as 30%.

5. Raise your co-pay.

This can lower your premium by as much as 30%.

6. Use your deductible carry-over credit.

You can carry over your expenses from this year to help meet the deductible for next year.

7. Lose weight.

Studies show that being obese adds an average of $395 to your costs. In fact, studies show that being obese adds more to the costs than smoking, aging and problem drinking.

8. Follow the rules of your plan.

If you are required to get a referral before seeing a specialist, for example, make sure you get it.

9. Follow the schedule.

Many plans will pay for annual procedures, such as gynecological exams, physicals, etc. Make sure you do not go in for a physical, for example, in less than 12 months from the previous one. Check your plan's "Schedule of Care" to see how often a specific procedure is covered.

10. Coordinate benefits with your spouse.

If your spouse is covered by an employer health plan insurance, depending on the premiums, you may be able to get more coverage or reduce your premium. Review both plans carefully before making your decision.

11. Avoid duplicate coverage.

Review your auto insurance policy to make sure you are not paying for the same coverage in both policies.

12. Track out-of-pocket expenses.

Many plans have a maximum out-of-pocket amount during a contract year. Keep a diary of your expenses to make sure you do not exceed the out-of-pocket limit.

13. Review your policy annually.

Make sure it still meets your family's needs.

14. Switch plans, if appropriate.

Many employer plans have an open enrollment period. However, if you find that your plan is not meeting your family's needs, contact your Human Resources Office and ask if you can switch to another plan, even if it is not during the open enrollment period.

15. Take reasonable risks.

If you are in good health and are not a big consumer of medical services, consider buying a "catastrophic" policy. By assuming a deductible as high as $2,500 you can cut your premium by as much as 50% or more.

Frequently Asked Questions:

Q. What is the first thing I should know about buying health coverage?

A. Your aim should be to insure yourself and your family against the most serious and financially disastrous losses that can result from an illness or accident. If you are offered health benefits at work, carefully review the plans' literature to make sure the one you select fits your needs. If you purchase individual coverage, buy a policy that will cover major expenses and pay them to the highest maximum level. Save money on premiums, if necessary, by taking large deductibles and paying smaller costs out-of-pocket.

Q. Can I buy a single health insurance policy that will provide all the benefits I'm likely to need?

A. No. Although you can select a plan or buy a policy that should cover most medical, hospital, surgical, and pharmaceutical bills, no single policy covers everything. Moreover, you may want to consider additional single-purpose policies like long-term care or disability income insurance. If you are over 65, you may want a Medicare supplemental policy to fill in the gaps in Medicare coverage.

Q. I'm planning to keep working after age 65. Will I be covered by Medicare or by my company's health insurance?

A. If you work for a company with 20 or more employees, your employer must offer you (through age 69) the same health insurance coverage offered to younger employees. After you reach age 65, you may choose between Medicare and your company's plan as your primary insurer. If you elect to remain in the company plan, it will pay first—for all benefits covered under the plan—before Medicare is billed. In most instances, it is to your advantage to accept continued employer coverage. But be sure to enroll in Medicare Part A, which covers hospitalization and can supplement your group coverage at no additional cost to you. You can save on Medicare premiums by not enrolling in Medicare Part B until you finally retire. Bare in mind, though, that delayed enrollment is more expensive and entails a waiting period for coverage.

Q. I've had a serious health condition that appears to be stabilized. Can I buy individual health coverage?

A. Depending on what your condition is and when it was diagnosed and treated, you can probably buy health coverage. However, the insurer may do one of three things:

o Provide full protection but with a higher premium, as might be the case with a chronic disease, such as diabetes;

o Modify the benefits to increase the deductible;

o Exclude the specific medical problem from coverage, if it is a clearly defined condition, as long as the insurer abides by state and federal laws on exclusions.

Q. One of my medical bills was turned down by the insurance company (or health plan). Is there anything I can do?

A. Ask the insurance company why the claim was rejected. If the answer is that the service isn't covered under your policy, and you're sure that it is covered, check to see that the provider entered the correct diagnosis or procedure code on the insurance claim form. Also check that your deductible was correctly calculated. Make sure that you didn't skip an essential step under your plan, such as pre admission certification. If everything is in order, ask the insurer to review the claim.

9

Get a degree without debt

According to a 1999 National Postsecondary Student Aid Study:

- o 60 percent of the students who completed a bachelor's degree in a four-year, public institution borrowed at least some of the money.

- o The median amount they borrowed was $15,375.

However, relying too heavily on loans (with the associated interest) is costly and can burden you with large debts just when you are working to establish your financial independence. Here are some tips for getting a college degree without being burdened with loans:

1. Calculate the cost.

If you already know which school you will attend:

- o Contact them to determine the cost for tuition, fees, and room and board.

- o Add 6 percent for inflation for each year between now and when you will enroll.

If you do not know which school you will attend go to: **www. finaid.org/calculators/costprojector.phtml**

- o Enter the average of $12,641 if you intend to enroll in a public college within your state or $19,188 if you plan to enroll in a public college out of state or $27,677 if you plan to enroll in a private college.

- o Add 6% for inflation.

- o Write in the number of years until you enroll.

- o Hit "Calculate".

2. Understand commonly used financial aid terms:

Award Letter — An official document from a college or other financial aid sponsor that lists all of the financial aid being offered to the student. The letter provides details explaining how the student's financial need was determined, describes the details of the financial aid package (amount, source, and type of aid), and discusses the terms and conditions attached to the financial aid award.

Award Year — The academic year for which financial aid is requested or awarded.

College Costs — Also referred to as the "cost of attendance," or COA. College costs refer to the total amount a student will pay to attend college, including tuition and fees, books and supplies, housing, meals, transportation, and personal expenses (laundry, health insurance, etc.)

Dependent — For an individual to be considered your dependent, they must live with you, and you must provide them with more than half their financial support. Spouses do not count as dependents in the Federal Methodology.

Dependent Student — A student dependent on his or her parents for financial support.

Early Decision — Early decision plans have earlier deadlines and earlier notification dates than the regular admissions process, and are geared for applicants who are sure of and likely to be accepted by the college they want to attend. A student who applies to a school through the early decision program commits to attending that school if admitted. The drawback -- students must accept the offer of admission before they find out about their financial aid package. You can apply early decision to only one school. You should only participate in an early decision program if the school is your first choice, and you don't want to consider other schools.

Electronic Student Aid Report (ESAR) — An electronic form of the Student Aid Report.

Expected Family Contribution (EFC) — The amount of money a family is expected to be able to contribute to a student's education, as determined by the Federal Methodology need analysis formula. The calculation takes into account taxable and nontaxable income, assets (i.e., savings and checking accounts), benefits (i.e., unemployment, Social Security, or alimony payments), student's dependency status, family size, and number of family members in college. The EFC includes both the parent and student contributions. The EFC is used in determining eligibility for federal, need-based aid by subtracting the EFC from the cost of attendance to determine the student's financial need. Unusual circumstances such as loss of employment, high medical expenses, or the death of a parent may affect your ability to pay for your education and should be brought to the attention of your school's financial aid advisor. He or she may be able to adjust the COA or EFC to compensate.

Federal Methodology — The Federal Methodology is the need analysis formula used to determine the Expected Family Contribution (EFC). It takes into account taxable and nontaxable income, assets, family size, and the number of family members in college. Unlike many Institutional Methodologies, it does not consider the net value of a family's home.

Financial Aid — Money provided to a student and/or his or her family to help pay for the student's education. Financial aid can be in the form of gift aid (grants and scholarships) or self-help aid (loans and work-study).

Financial Aid Package — The total financial aid award received by a student from all sources (federal, state, institutional, and private). The financial aid package is likely to be made up of a combination of aid (grants, loans, scholarships, and work-study). Unsubsidized Stafford loans and PLUS loans are not considered part of the financial aid package, since they are available to the family to help meet the Expected Family Contribution.

Financial Need — The amount by which a student's resources (family contribution) falls short of covering the student's cost of attending school, usually defined as the difference between the Cost of Attendance (COA) and the *Expected Family Contribution (EFC)*. A student's financial aid package is based on financial need, as established by the need analysis. Assessments of need may differ, depending on the need analysis methodology used (i.e. federal vs. institutional).

Free Application for Federal Student Aid (FAFSA) — A form used to apply for Pell Grants and all other need-based aid. An electronic form of the FAFSA called the FAFSA Express is also available. There is no charge for completing the FAFSA. In many states, completion of the FAFSA is also sufficient for establishing eligibility for state-sponsored aid programs.

Gift Aid — Student financial aid that does not have to be repaid and that does not require the recipient to be employed (for example, grants and scholarships).

Grants and scholarships — also known as gift aid, do not have to be repaid. Grants are usually awarded on the basis of need alone, while scholarships may have certain requirements that must be met, such as maintaining excellent grade-point averages, participating in certain activities, or completing specific courses.

Gross Income — Income before taxes, deductions, and allowances have been subtracted.

Income — The amount of money received from employment (salary, wages, tips), profit from financial instruments (interest, dividends, capital gains), or other sources (child support, Social Security, pensions, disability).

Institutional Methodology — A formula, other than the federal methodology, used by a college or university to determine financial need for the al location of said school's financial aid funds.

Merit-based aid — Financial aid that is awarded based on a student's academic, athletic, or artistic merit, or some other criteria, and does not depend on the existence of financial need. Merit-based awards may look at a student's grades, test scores, special talents, or extra-curricular actives (volunteer activities, clubs, and hobbies) to determine eligibility.

Methodologies — Need analysis formulas used to determine eligibility for student aid. There are three financial aid methodologies: the Federal Methodology, the Institutional Methodologies, and the Simplified Methodology (or Simplified Need Test).

Need — The difference between cost of college attendance and a student's (and the student's parents') ability to pay that cost. Cost of attendance - Expected family contribution = Financial need

Need Analysis — The process that determines a student's financial need by analyzing the financial information provided by the student and his or her parents (or spouse, if applicable) on a financial aid form. The need analysis is the first step in applying for financial aid. All students must file a Free Application for Federal Aid (FAFSA) to apply for need-based federal financial aid programs. Some schools, particularly private colleges, also require students to fill out other forms (see institutional methodology) for aid funded by that college. For state financial aid programs, the FAFSA may or may not be the only form a student needs to submit. Check with your state agency to find out if any other application form is needed.

Need-based aid — Financial aid that is awarded based on a student's financial situation. Most government student financial aid is need-based. Need-based aid can be awarded in the form of grants, loans, or work-study pay. One of the principles of need-based financial aid is that students (and their families) should pay for educational expenses to the extent they are able. Students who think their educational expenses will be higher than they or their families can afford should apply for need-based aid. You don't have to be poor to qualify for financial aid, but you do have to apply if you want to get it.

Need-blind — In need-blind admissions, a school decides whether to offer admission to a student without considering the student's financial situation.

Out-of-State Student — A student who does not meet the residency requirements for the state. State public colleges and universities often charge out-of-state students a higher tuition rate.

Parent Contribution — The amount a student's parents are expected to pay toward college expenses from their income and assets. The amount is determined by a need analysis. Some of the factors considered in this calculation are income, the number of parents earning income, assets, family size, and the number of family members currently attending college. The Parent Contribution and the Student Contribution together constitute the Expected Family Contribution.

Pell Grants — A federally sponsored and administered grant program that provides funds of up to $2,340 to undergraduate students, based on the student's financial need. Congress sets the dollar range of the Pell Grant annually.

Postsecondary — "After high school." Refers to all programs for high school graduates.

Priority Dates — Timeframes set by colleges that students should try to follow when filing the FAFSA. Students filing by the priority date of a particular school have a better chance of receiving the most possible financial aid from that school. If you miss the priority date, you can still receive financial aid, but the amount may be less or the aid may be in a different form (perhaps a higher loan ratio) than if you had filed earlier.

ROTC — Reserve Officers' Training Corps program. A scholarship program in which the military pays most of the cost of tuition, fees, and textbooks, and also provides a monthly allowance. In return, scholarship recipients are expected to participate in summer training while in college and fulfill a service commitment after college.

Scholarship — A form of gift aid. Like a grant, a scholarship does not have to be paid back. Most scholarships are restricted to paying all or part of tuition expenses, although a few also cover room and board. Scholarships usually come from private sources, such as civic and religious groups or individual schools, although there are some state and federal scholarships. Scholarships are usually awarded based on merit as opposed to financial need.

Scholastic Assessment Test (SAT I) — The SAT is one of two national standardized college entrance examinations use in the United States. The other is the ACT.

Self-help Aid — Aid in the form of loans and student employment. In other words, unlike grants and scholarships, it's not free.

Service Academy — A four-year college that offers a bachelor's degree and commission in the military. Service academies -- which include the U.S. Air Force Academy, U.S. Coast Guard Academy, U.S. Merchant Marine Academy, U.S. Military Academy, and U.S. Naval Academy -- are highly selective, and students must be nominated by their congressional representative in order to apply.

Simplified Methodology (Simplified Need Test) — Need analysis used by families whose total adjusted gross incomes are under $50,000 and who are eligible to file a 1040EZ, 1040A, or who do not file a tax return. (In the case of independent students, the same criteria is applied to the student and, if applicable, the student's spouse.) The Simplified Methodology is essentially the same as the Federal Methodology, except the Simplified Methodology does not count either parent or student assets in the Expected Family Contribution calculation.

Student Aid Report (SAR) — The SAR summarizes the information included in the FAFSA and contains your expected family contribution (EFC). When you receive your SAR, check it for any mistakes. If you find a mistake, make the correction(s) on Part 2 of the form and return it to the processor in the envelope provided. If there aren't any mistakes, and if you did not receive the report electronically, copy the form for your records and send the original to your school's financial aid office.

Supplemental Education Opportunity Grant (SEOG) — A federal grant program that helps undergraduates with exceptional financial need. SEOGs are awarded by the school's financial aid office and provide up to $4,000 a year. To qualify, a student must also be a recipient of a Pell Grant.

Tuition — The amount of money colleges charge for instruction and use of facilities. Room, board, and fees are charged in addition to tuition, so the terms "tuition" and "costs" are not synonymous.

Work Study — Another form of self-help aid. The Federal Work-Study Program is probably the most familiar example of this type of program, although many colleges may offer similar programs. Work-study aid is money a student must earn by working a part-time job, usually at the college or university the student is attending or at a nonprofit organization.

3. Start a savings program.

a. Buy U.S. Savings Bonds (Series EE, Series I).

In 1990, The Treasury Department announced the "Education Bond Program". This program allows interest to be completely or partially excluded from federal income tax when the bond owner pays qualified education expenses at an eligible institution or pays into a state tuition plan in the same calendar year the bonds are redeemed.

For further information, see IRS Publication 970 — Tax Benefits for Education.

You can also get information at **www.publicdebt.treas.gov.**

b. Contribute to a Qualified Tuition Program (QTP).

Sometimes known as a Section 529 Plans, there are two types of QTPs: Prepaid Tuition Plans and College Savings Plans.

1) Prepaid Tuition Plans — These are usually offered by the state in which you live. The parent has to either deposit enough today to cover the plan cost or arrange a time payment plan. Either way, the parent is contracting to put enough money aside to cover the cost of the plan. The state guarantees tuition money equivalent to the cost of its state schools tuition. These plans offer several advantages:

o   You can lock in tuition at the current rates.
o   Plans are guaranteed by the full faith and credit of your state.
o   The investment risk is low.
o   The return is generally better than a bank savings account and certificate of deposit.
o   The plans may be exempt from federal taxes.
o   You may be able to claim a tax deduction on your state tax return.

All 50 states (including Washington, DC) now offer prepaid tuition plans. Since every state's plan has its own rules go to **www.collegesavings.org** and click on "Your State" to find out how your state plan works.

Prepaid tuition plans are not for everyone. They mostly attract middle-income families who tend to be more conservative in their investments. If you are a lower-income family and use this option, you may jeopardize your chances for state aid and you may forfeit money you need for immediate essentials. However, if your state offers a plan and you are interested:

o Make sure it covers the cost of tuition, room and board.
o Check to see if it applies to other than state schools.
o Confirm that your original deposit will be returned if your child attends a private or an out-of-state college, is not accepted at a state school or chooses not to attend college at all.

For more information refer to IRS Publication 970 - Tax Benefits for Education.

2) College Savings Plans — Unlike the prepaid tuition plan, the College Savings Plans do not guarantee that the student will have enough money to pay for college. Whether or not there is sufficient money available to meet the college expenses depends on the plan's investment returns. The advantages College Savings Plans are:

o They have little impact on eligibility for financial aid.
o Students can attend any college.
o If your child does not go to college, the money can be used for another family member's qualified education expenses or you may keep the money and be taxed at your rate plus a 10% penalty.

www.savingforcollege.com gives a rating of various Section 529 plans and provides an overview of tax, gift and account control issues of the plans.

c. Open a Coverdell Education Savings Account.

Parents can set up these accounts with after-tax dollars to pay the qualified educational expenses for a child under age 18. Three big advantages:

1) It is free of federal taxation when you withdraw money from the account to pay qualified educational expenses.

2) You have a lot of flexibility in how to invest in these accounts. You can open an account at a bank, with a stockbroker or directly with a mutual fund company.

3) Contributions limits were increased to $2,000 per beneficiary in 2002.

For further information, see IRS Publication 970 — Tax Benefits for Education.

4. Enroll in a Rewards Program.

a. Upromise —

This is a free service in which businesses give you money back that you can use to pay for your children's education. Their motivation is to earn your loyalty. Here is how it works:

- o You designate a recipient of the reward program. It can be your child, grandchild, a friend's child or maybe a child that you expect to have someday.
- o You register your credit card.
- o Each time you make a purchase at that store using the registered credit card, the store credits a percentage of the purchase price to the beneficiary's account.

Presently, there are over 100 stores and over 900 restaurants offering contributions.

To get an up-to-date list of participating businesses and to get more information go to **www.upromise.com.**

b. Babymint —

Like Upromise, Babymint is a free service that gives participants a reward for their loyalty. Here is how it works:

o   You get a Babymint credit card and register it.
o   You designate a savings account for your child or yourself.
o   As you, your friends, the grandparents and anyone else you can recruit make purchases, the business directs a rebate into your designated account.

For more information go to **www.babymint.com**

c. Tuition Rewards Program—

With this program, over 150 colleges and universities give matching rebates in the form of reduced tuition if your child attends one of the participating schools.

For more information and to get a list participating colleges, go to **www.tuitionrewards.com**

5. Reduce the cost.

There are several steps you can take to lower the cost of your college education:

a. Enroll in a cooperative education program.

Combine going to school with working in your major field of study. As an example, you may work for a semester and go to school for a semester. It will take longer to complete the degree, but in the end you will have hands-on experience, a potential job offer and no loans. Visit your local library and get a copy of the Directory of College Cooperative Education Programs. This directory, which is published by the National Commission on Cooperative Education, lists over 460 colleges that offer cooperative programs.

b. Attend a community college and transfer to a 4-year school.

You save money on room and board while earning vital college credits that cost less than they would at a four-year school. Get a written commitment from the four-year college to which you plan to transfer stating that they will accept your credits.

c. Accelerate your degree program.

Look for schools that will allow you to complete your degree in less than four years. Many schools have programs in which you can cram a semester's worth of work into six-eight weeks. Other schools have different types of time and money-saving options. For example, Seton Hall College in Greensburg, PA allows students to complete course work for a Bachelor's Degree and a Master's degree in Elementary Education for the cost of a bachelor's degree.

d. Take advance placement (AP) courses.

Taking AP courses and passing the appropriate tests reduces the number of courses you have to take (and pay for) once you enroll in college. Check with your high school guidance counselor or with the college admissions office for eligibility requirements and program specifics. You can also check **www.collegeboard. com/ap/students**

e. Stay in state.

Many schools charge out-of-state students much more than they do in-state students. As an example, during the 2001-2002 academic year, a North Carolina resident paid $3,184 for tuition at the University of North Carolina at Chapel Hill
while an out-of-state student paid $12,350

f. Use CLEP.

The College-Level Examination Program (CLEP) gives students an opportunity to demonstrate college level knowledge they have gained through independent study, advanced high school courses, or noncredit courses. You take an exam (which costs approximately $50), and if you pass it you do not have to take that course in college. For more information go to **www. collegeboard.com/student/testing/clep/about.html**

g. Attend the school where your parents work.

Many schools offer a free education in the form of tuition remission to employees' children.

h. Use tuition exchange.

If your parents work for a college but you want to attend another college, there are over 500 colleges that have set aside money for tuition exchange. That means that you get the same tuition remission as you would at the college at which your parents work. For more details go to **www.tuitionexchange.org**

i. Commute.

Save thousands on room and board by living at home.

j. Attend mom or Dad's alma mater.

Some schools offer a partial tuition remission for children of alumni.

k. Participate in extracurricular activities.

Attend a school that gives a tuition reduction for having served as student government president, editor of the newspaper, etc.

l. Seek multiple child discounts.

Some schools offer a discount if more than one child from the same family is attending.

m. Recruit another student.

Some schools will offer a tuition reduction if you recruit another student.

n. Take summer classes.

These extra credits hasten your graduation day, thus cutting tuition costs.

o. Earn room and board as resident assistant.

p. Look for a tuition-free school.

Believe it or not, there are schools that do not charge tuition. You may have to work in your major, but you end up with a college degree and no loans. Some tuition-free schools are:

Webb Institute, Glen Cove, NY

They offer degrees in naval Architecture and marine engineering. Their web site is **www.webb-institute.edu**.

Moody Bible College, Chicago, ILL

They offer a bachelor's degree in Christian Ministry and missionary aviation which includes flight training. Their web site is **www.moody.edu**.

Berea College, Kentucky

They offer degrees in 26 majors. The web site is **www.berea. edu**.

College of the Ozarks, Missouri

They provide endowments and other financial aid to cover tuition cost. Their web site is **www.cofo.edu**.

Curtis Institute of Music, Philadelphia, PA

They offer a music degree.
Their web site is **www.curtis.edu**.

Alice Lloyd College, KY
Their web site is **www.alc.edu**.

Cooper Union, New York
They offer degrees in art, engineering and architecture.
The web site is **www.cooper.edu**.

q. Seek a referral from an alumni member.

If you know someone who is active in the alumni association of the school you want to attend, ask them to give you a referral. This sometimes comes with a reduction in tuition.

6. Look for grants.

Some examples are:

a. Pell

- o The largest federal grant program.
- o Awarded to students on the basis of need.
- o In 2003 the amounts of the awards ranged from $400 - $4,050.

- o Factors that determine the amount of the award are: the college's costs, the estimated family contribution and whether or not the student attends part-time or full time.
- o Eligibility is determined by the Department of Education after the student completes the Free Application for Federal Student Aid (FAFSA).

For further information, see the high school guidance counselor or the college financial aid office.

b. Federal Supplemental Education Opportunity (FSEO)

- o Awarded to students based on need.
- o Students who receive a Pell Grant receive priority for being awarded an FSEOG Grant.
- o The award ranges from $100 - $5,000 per year.
- o Students can apply at the college financial aid office.

c. Leveraging Educational Assistance Partnership (LEAP), formerly known as State Student Incentive Grants (SSI)

- o Funded by individual states and the federal government.
- o The average award is $1,000.
- o College financial aid advisors and high school counselors notify students if they qualify.

7. Look for scholarships.

Some places to look are:

a. The high school guidance office.

Find out if they have a list of scholarships awarded to former students. This may help you target your search.

b. The college financial aid office.

Some colleges offer scholarships and grants from their own resources.

c. The college academic department.

Someone in the department may know of scholarships available to students pursuing your major field of study.

d. Professors in your department.

They may have contacts that can lead to scholarships.

e. The military.

The military offers numerous opportunities to both serve your country and get a free education. Some examples are:

1) The Montgomery G. I. Bill.

You can qualify for money for college at any two or four-year college, vocational school, or correspondence course. You commit to full-time duty (usually for four years, but there are also 2, 3 and 6-year programs) with one branch of the military. While serving, you can qualify for college money by contributing $100 per month for 12 months ($1,200 total) through payroll deduction. You are then eligible for $536 a month for 36 months for a total of $19,296. You can use this money as a part-time student while serving on active duty, or as a full-time student after completing your active duty. For further information go to **www.gibill.va.gov**.

2) Your state National Guard.

The reserve component of the Montgomery G.I. Bill allows you to serve in the military branch of your choice on a part-time basis (usually two weeks a year and one weekend per month for

93

six years). During that time, you can earn up to $9,180 in total benefits. Unlike being on active duty, the reserve component does not require you to contribute any money to your benefits. You become eligible for up to $255 a month for up to 36 months after you complete basic and technical training. You can attend class full-time while you serve. The Army and Air National Guard require the same commitment of time (six years) as the reserves and provide the same amount of college money (up to $9,180). However, you may also be entitled to additional state money for college. You may even be eligible for up to full tuition at some state schools.

For further information, visit the Air National Guard at **www. ang.af.mil** and the Army National Guard at **www.arng.army. mil**.

3) The Air Force Community College.

The Community College of the Air Force, an accredited two-year college, offers more that 70 associate degree programs in scientific and technical fields, free of charge for Air Force enlisted personnel. For further information go to **www.au.af. mil/au/ccaf/index.htm**.

4) Reserve Officers Training Corps (ROTC).

The Army, Navy, Air Force and Marines offer these programs at select colleges and universities throughout the country. If you qualify, the ROTC program offers a unique college experience. During the first two years you can attend ROTC classes, such as military science, and participate in training activities, all with no obligation. During your junior and senior years, you may receive a full scholarship, including tuition, books, room and board and other expenses. This, of course, requires a commitment to serve as an officer for a minimum of three years after graduation. For further information, go to:

Navy and Marine ROTC at **www.nrotc.navy.mil/**.

Army ROTC at **www.armyrotc.com/**.

Air Force ROTC at **www.afrotc.com**.

5) Service Academies.

Except for the Marines, each branch of the military has an academy. Each offers a free college education in exchange for your willingness to serve in the military for a predetermined number of years. You can get information directly from each academy:

U.S. Military Academy at West Point (Army) at **www.usma. edu**.

U.S. Naval Academy at **www.usna.edu**.

U.S. Air Force at **www.usafa.af.mil**.

U.S. Coast Guard Academy at **www.cga.edu**.

U.S. Merchant Marine Academy at **www.usmm.edu**.

f. Your parents' employer.

Some employers offer scholarships to employees' children. Check with your parents' company Human Resources Department to see if they offer scholarships, to find out about the eligibility requirements and the application procedure.

g. Your parents' labor union.

As a way to support their members, many unions give scholarships to member's children. Some examples are:

National Alliance of Postal and Federal Employees at **www.napfe.com**.

Postal Employees Educational Assistance Fund at **www.feea.gov**.

Communication Workers of America at **www.aflcio.org**.

National Association of Letter Carriers at **www.nalc.org**.

Service Employees International Union at **www.aflcio.org**.

American Federal of Teachers at **www.aflcio.org**.

Bricklayers and Allied Craft Workers at **www.aflcio.org**.

For a complete list of scholarships, get the AFL-CIO Guide to Union-Sponsored Scholars, Awards and Student Aid at **www.aflcio.org**.

h. Your state.

Each state has programs to help pay for college. Visit your state's web site to determine programs for which you are eligible.

Alabama
Alabama Commission on Higher Education
www.ache.state.al.us

Alaska
Alaska Commission on Postsecondary Education
www.state.ak.us/acpe/

Arizona
Arizona Commission for Postsecondary Education
www.acpe.asu.edu

Arkansas
Arkansas Department of Higher Education
www.aekansashighered.com

California
California Student Aid Commission
www.csac.ca.gov

Colorado
Colorado Commission on Higher Education
www.state.co.us/cche/

Connecticut
Connecticut Department of Higher Education
www.ctdhe.org

Delaware
Delaware Higher Education Commission
www.doe.state.de.us/high-ed/

District of Columbia
State Education Office of District of Columbia
www.seo.dc.gov

Florida
Florida Department of Education
www.floridastudentfinancialaid.org

Georgia
Georgia Student Finance Authority
www.gsfc.org

Hawaii
Hawaii State Postsecondary Education Commission
www.hern.hawaii.edu/hern/

Idaho
Idaho State Board of Education
www.idahoboardofed.org

Illinois
Illinois Student Assistance Commission
www.isac-online.org

Indiana
State Student Assistance Commission of Indiana
www.in.gov/ssaci/

Iowa
Iowa College Student Aid Commission
www.iowacoolegeaid.org

Kansas
Kansas Board of Regents
www.kansasregents.org

Kentucky
Kentucky Higher Education Assistance Authority
www.kheaa.com

Louisiana
Louisiana Office of Student Financial Assistance
www.osfa.state.la.us

Maine
Maine Education Assistance Division Finance Authority of Maine
www.famemaine.com

Maryland
Maryland Higher Education Commission
www.mhec.state.md.md.us

Massachusetts
Massachusetts Office of Student Financial Assistance
www.osfa.mass.edu

Michigan
Michigan Higher Education Assistance Authority
www.michigan.gov/mistudentaid/

Minnesota
Minnesota Higher Education Services Office
www.mheso.state.mn.us

Mississippi
Mississippi Office of Student Financial Aid
www.ihl.state.ms.us

Missouri
Missouri Department of Higher Education
www.cbhe.state.mo.us

Montana
Student Assistance Foundation of Montana
www.safmt.org

Nebraska
Nebraska Coordinating Commission for Postsecondary Education
www.ccpe.state.ne.us

Nevada
Nevada Department of Education
www.nde.state.nv.us

New Hampshire
New Hampshire Postsecondary Education Commission
www.state.nh.us/postsecondary/

New Jersey
Higher Education Student Assistance Authority
www.hesaa.org

New Mexico
New Mexico Commission on Higher Education
www.nmche.org/

New York
New York State Higher Education Services Corporation
www.hesc.com

North Carolina
North Carolina State Education Assistance Authority
www.ncseaa.edu

North Dakota
North Dakota Student Financial Assistance Program
www.ndus.edu

Ohio
Ohio Department of Education
www.ode.state.oh.us

Oklahoma
Oklahoma State Regents for Higher Education
www.okhighered.org

Oregon
Oregon Student Assistance Commission
www.getcollegefunds.org

Pennsylvania
Pennsylvania Higher Education Assistance Agency
www.pheaa.org

Rhode Island
Rhode Island Higher Education Assistance Authority
www.riheaa.org

South Carolina
South Carolina Commission on Higher Education
www.che400.state.sc.us

South Dakota
South Dakota Department of Education and Cultural Affairs
www.state.sf.us/deca/

Tennessee
Tennessee Higher Education Commission
www.state.tn.us/thec/

Texas
Texas Higher Education Coordinating Board
www.thccb.state.tx.us

Utah
Utah Higher Education Assistance Authority
www.uheaa.org

Vermont
Vermont Student Assistance Corporation
www.vsac.org

Virginia
State Council of Higher Education for Virginia
www.schev.edu

Washington
Washington State Higher Education Coordinating Board
www.hecb.wa.gov

West Virginia
West Virginia Higher Education Policy Commission
www.hepc.wvnet.edu

Wisconsin
Wisconsin Higher Educational Aids Board
www.heab.state.wi.us

Wyoming
Wyoming Department of Education
www.ky.wy.us

i. Organizations that offer scholarships based on extracurricular activities.

Examples are:

Boy Scouts of America at **www.scouting.org**.

Girl Scouts at **www.girlscouts.org**.

Boys and Girls Club at **www.bgca.org**.

Future Farmers of America at **www.ffa.org**.

Junior Achievement at **www.ja.org**.

National Forensics League **www.debate.uvm.edu/NFL/nflhome.html**.

j. Fraternities and Sororities.

Check with the local and national organization to find out about scholarships and the application procedure.

k. Local service clubs.

These are examples of organizations that view sponsoring scholarships as a way of serving the community:

American Legion at **www.legion.org**.

Elks Club at **www.elks.org**.

Optimist International at **www.optimist.org**.

Rotary at **www.rotarty.org**.

l. Churches/religious organizations.

A number of church/religious organizations provide scholarships. Some examples are the:

American Baptist Church at **www.abcem.org**.

Assemblies of God at **www.ag.org**.

Catholic Church at **www.catholicaid.com**.

Evangelical Lutheran Church at **www.elca.org**

Presbyterian Church at **www.pcusa.org**.

Methodist Church at **www.umc.org**.

United Church of Christ **www.ucc.org**.

m. Professional Associations.

These organizations give scholarships to students pursuing education that leads to a career in the respective field:

American Bar Association at **www.abanet.org/lsd/.**

American Criminal Justice Association at **www.acjalae.org**.

American Society of Mechanical Engineers at **www.asme.org**.

American Society of Women Accountants at **www.aswa.org**

Association for Women in Mathematics at **www.awm-math. org.**

Association for Women in Science at **www.awis.org**.

National Restaurant Association at **www.restaurant.org**

National Society of Accountants at **www.nsacct.org**.

National Student Nurses' Association at **www.nsna.org**.

n. Local businesses.

Many local businesses give back to the community by offering scholarships. Check with your local Chamber of Commerce for a list of businesses. If you have a part-time job, ask the manager if the company has a scholarship program.

o. National businesses.

Many national businesses give scholarships as a way of giving back to the community. Some examples are:

Coca-cola gives away over $2,000,000 annually. Awards are based on academic achievement, character, and leadership. Visit them at **www.coca-colascholarship.org**.

Microsoft gives scholarships to students interested in studying software development. Visit them at **www.microsoft.com/ college/scholarships/**.

Papa Johns gives scholarships based on academic achievement, character, life goals and interests. Visit them at **www.papajohns. com**.

Wal-Mart gives scholarships based on students' participation in their community. Visit them at **www.walmartfoundation.org**.

Sears gives scholarships based on community service and extra curricular activities. The National Hot Rod Association administers the scholarship program. Visit them at **www.nhra. com/aboutnhr/youth.htm**.

Toyota gives scholarship based on leadership and community service. Their web site is **www.toyota.com/ communityscholars**.

Tylenol gives scholarships to students who have shown leadership in the community and want to pursue a career in health care. Their web site is **www.tylenolscholarship.com**.

p. Free scholarship search services such as:

www.fastweb.org
   o   They have a database of over 600,000 scholarships worth over 1 billion dollars.

www.collegeboard.com
   o   They have a database of over 2,300 scholarship sources totaling nearly 3 billion dollars in aid.

www.wiredscholar.com
- o They connect you to over 2.4 million wards worth over 14 billion dollars. The database is updated daily.

q. The career you intent to pursue.

Examples are:

Education
- o The American Mensa Education and Research Foundation offers scholarship to undergraduate students seeking to become teachers. Their telephone number is 817-332-2600.
- o Phi Delta Kappa offers scholars to students seeking to become teachers. Their telephone number is 800-766-1156.
- o The Paul Douglas Teacher Scholarship Program is available in some states to help outstanding academic achievers pursue teaching careers.

Engineering
- o American Society for Engineering at **www.tech-interns. com** provides fellowship opportunities in engineering, science and technology for undergraduate and graduate students.

Environment
- o The Environmental Protection Agency offers internships, scholarships and fellowships to students interested in pursing a degree dealing with the environment. Their web site is **www.epa.go/students/career.htm.**

Government Service
- o The Truman Scholarship Foundation awards scholarships for students to attend undergraduate and professional schools in preparation for careers in government. Their web site is **www.truman.gov**.

Health Care
- o The Department of Health and Human Services provides a variety of scholarships to students in the health profession. The web site is **www.bhpr.hrsa.gov/dsa/index.htm.**

Math, Science and Engineering
- o The Barry M. Goldwater Scholarship and Excellence in Education Program was created to offer scholarships to encourage outstanding students to pursue a career in math, sciences or engineering. Their web site is **www.act.org/goldwater.**

Medicine
- o The National Institute of Health offers scholarships to students study medicine. Their web site is **www.nhsc.gov.**

Nursing
- o The National League for Nursing provides scholarship to students interested in becoming a nurse. Their web site is **www.nln.org.**

Science
- o The National Science Foundation offers scholarships to students pursuing a career in science. Their web site is **www.nsf.gov/home/grants.htm.**

Space
- o The National Aeronautics and Space Administration offers scholarships for people pursuing a degree in space. Their web site is **www.nasa.gov/audience/forstudents/ postsecondary.**

Veterinary Medicine
- o The Department of Agriculture offers scholarships to students pursuing a degree in veterinary medicine. Their web site is **www.aphis.usda.gov/mb/mrphr/jobs/stw. html.**

r. Organization that award scholarships based on race and ethnicity.

Some examples are:

The League of United Latin American Citizens (LULAC) at **www.lulac.org/programs/centers.html** offers scholarships to Hispanic students.

www.minoritynurse.com offers a large listing of nursing scholarships available for minority nursing students.

The National Society of Black Engineers at **www.nsbe.org/** offers scholarships, internships in order to help increase the number of minority students studying engineering.

The National Association for the Advancement of Colored People (NAACP) at **www.naacp.org/work/education/eduschool** offers scholarships to African American and other minorities to help them achieve their educational goals.

The NAACP and the Department of Energy offers scholarships to students pursuing a degree in computer science. The NAACP web site is **www.naacp.org/work/education/eduscholar.shtml**.

The United Negro College Fund offers an enormous number of scholarships each year. Scholarships are awarded by major field of study, by achievement score, by classification and by state. Their web site is **www.uncf.org/scholarshipsearch.asp**.

The Congressional Black Caucus offers scholarships, internships and fellowships. Their web site is **www.cbcfinc.org/scholarship. html**.

The Gates Millennium Scholarship Program (GMS) offers scholarships to African Americans, American Indians/Alaska Natives, Asian and Hispanic Americans who are interested in studying mathematics, science, education or library science. Their web site is **www.gmsp.org**.

The Hispanic Scholarship Fund offers scholarships to Hispanic students. Their web site is **www.hsf.org**.

The Hispanic Heritage Awards Foundation awards scholarships to students studying math, science and engineering. Their web site is **www.hispanicawards.org**.

The Society of Hispanic Engineers offers scholarships to Hispanic students studying math and science. Their web site is **www.shpe.org**.

The Japanese American Citizens League offers several scholarships to students who have demonstrated a desire to excel. Their web site is **www.jacl.org.**.

The Thurgood Marshall Fund offers scholarships to students enrolled in a historically Black public college or university. Their web site is **www.thurgoodmarshallfund.org**.

The Ron Brown Scholarship Program provides scholarships to motivated African American students. For more information go to **www.ronbrown.org**.

The National Black Police Association offers scholarships to students studying law enforcement. Their web site is **www. blackpolice.org**.

The National Association of Black Journalists offers scholarships to African American students studying journalism. Their web site is **www.nabj.org**

The National Association of Minority Engineers offers scholarships to minority students studying engineering. Their web site is **www.namepa.org**.

The National Association of Black Accountants offers scholarships to African American students and others studying accounting. Their web site is **www.nabainc.org**.

Additional resources for minority students:

Barry Beckham, *The Black Student's Guide to Scholarships*, 4th edition, Madison Books, Lanham, MD, 1996. ISBN 1-56833-079-0 ($14.95). 150 pages. Lists more than 475 sources of private sector financial aid for black and minority students and provides tips on finding and applying for financial aid. To order, call 1-800-462-6420, send email to beckham@erols.com, or write to National Book Network, Inc., 4720 Boston Way, Lanham, MD 20706.

Lemuel Berry, Jr., *Minority Financial Aid Directory*, Kendall Hunt Publishers, 1995. ISBN 0-84039-944-8 ($45.95). Contains more than 4,000 listings of scholarships, fellowships, grants and loans for minority students.

Gail Ann Schlachter and R. David Webber, *Directory of Financial Aid for Minorities 1995-97*, Reference Service Press, San Carlos, CA 1995. ISBN 0-91827-628-4 ($47.50 plus $4 postage and handling). 600 pages. Includes more than 2,000 scholarships, fellowships, grants and loans for minority pre-doctoral and post-doctoral students, indexed according to type of minority. To place an order, call 1-415-594-0743, or write to Reference Service Press, 1100 Industrial Road, Suite #9, San Carlos, CA 94070.

U.S. Department of Education, *Higher Education Opportunities for Minorities and Women* -- Annotated Selections, U.S. Government Printing Office, 1996. ISBN 0-16-045218-X ($8.00). 105 pages. A list of opportunities for minority and female undergraduate, graduate and postdoctoral students, organized by academic area, with a separate list of general programs. Includes a bibliography. To order a copy, write to Superintendent of Documents, Mail Stop: SSOP, Washington, DC 20402-9328.

Evlene B. Wilson, *Money for College: A Guide to Financial Aid for African-American Students*, Penguin, New York, May 1996. ISBN 0-452-27276-9 ($15.95). 481 pages. Lists about 1,000 sources of financial aid for minority students, about 2/3 college-controlled and 1/3 from private sources, with a bit of information about federal student aid. Also includes a school index, field index and athletic award index. To order, write to Penguin Books USA, 375 Hudson Street, New York, NY 10014.

William C. Young, *The Higher Education Money Book for Minorities and Women,* Young, Matthews & Cox, Fairfax, Virginia, 1993. ISBN 0-9639490-0-4 ($23). A directory of scholarships, fellowships, grants and loans. To order, call 1-703-385-3065, fax 1-703-385-1839, or write to Young, Matthews & Cox, 10520 Warwick Avenue, Suite B-8, Fairfax, VA 22030-3136.

s. Organizations that award scholarships based on gender.

Some examples are:

The Society of Women Engineers (SWE) at **www.swe.org** offers scholarships to help women achieve their full potential in careers as engineers.

The Educational Foundation for Women in Accounting (EFWA) **www.efwa.org** offers scholarship to help women pursue careers in accounting.

Yale University at **www.yale.edu** has collected a list of organizations that provide financial help to undergraduate women studying computer science.

Tips for Winning Scholarships and grants:

a. Start Early.

Since the competition is keen, and since organizations offering grants and scholarships have deadlines, you should start your search 18-24 months before entering college.

b. Prepare your eligibility profile.

Since many scholarships are very specific, this is a critical first step in narrowing your search for scholarships, fellowships and grants for which you might be eligible. When you make your eligibility profile indicate such things as: where you are from, potential majors, grade point average, extracurricular activities, community service, organizations and clubs to which you belong, leadership positions held, ethnic background, religious affiliation and sports involvement. When it comes time to provide this information on an application or in an interview, you will have it at your fingertips. My niece, for example, received a scholarship that was only available to a Black female from the Eastern Shore of Virginia who was attending the University of Virginia.

c. Complete an FAFSA.

FAFSA, which stands for Free Application for Federal Student Aid, is the starting point for determining your need for financial aid. You should complete this 18-24 months before enrolling. You can get a copy of the application at **www.studentaid.ed.gov**, from a high school guidance counselor or the local library. If you prefer, you can complete the form online at **www.fafsa.ed.gov**.

d. Research the organization thoroughly.

Identify key words, their mission and values. When you submit your application include these key words, values and mission in your application package.

e. Read, understand and follow the application instructions.

If something is not clear, contact the organization for clarification.

f. Identify the deadline for application and submit yours early.

g. Tell the truth about extra curricular activities, grades, memberships, family finances and any other information you submit.

h. Ask at least three people to write a letter of recommendation to include in your application package, even if the application does not require it.

i. List your accomplishments.

Stress leadership roles you have taken. Scholarship committees love leadership.

j. If possible, interview others who have received a scholarship from the organization.

Ask what worked for them.

k. Look for ways to make your application stand out.

Send a video of you on the debate team, for example.

l. Write from the scholarship committee's perspective.

Ask yourself, "Why should the committee award me a scholarship"?

m. Proofread your application before submitting it.

n. Follow up to make sure the scholarship committee received your application.

o. Send a "Thank-you "note when you receive notification of your award.

This can be extremely helpful in getting your scholarship renewed in subsequent years.

8. Look for internships that provide a stipend or pays tuition.

Some fields in which this internships are available and the organizations that offer them are:

a. Aircraft and technology.

Lockheed Martin offers internships to students pursuing a degree in such disciples as management information systems, computer science, mechanical engineer, and electrical engineering. For more information, visit their web site at **www.lockheedmartin. com/manassas/html/**

b. Clothing Design.

Liz Claiborne offers summer internships in New York and Los Angeles. For more information go to **www.lizclaiborne.com**

c. Hospitality.

Marriott offers internships for students who are pursuing a degree in any phase of the hospitality industry. For more information, contact them at **www.marriott.com**

d. Research.

The National Institutes of Health provides internships during the summer at all of their locations. For more information, go to **www.training.nih.gov/student/**

e. Space.

Students studying such subjects as aerospace engineering, mechanical, electrical engineering and math can apply for internships to split their time between classroom work and working (and getting paid) at Johnson Space Flight Center.

For more information, go to **www.coop.jsc.nasa.gov**

9. Look for work-study programs.

The federal Work-Study Program allows students who have a financial need to work either on campus or in the community in order to pay for their education. The college financial aid office can provide details once you have completed the FAFSA (Free Application for Federal Student Aid).

10. Get your loans forgiven.

a. Teach in a low-income school.

If you received a Stafford Loan after 1998 and teach in a low - income school for 5 years you may be eligible to have up to $5,000 of your loan cancelled.

If you received a Perkins Loan prior to June 23, 1992 and teach full-time in a low-income school on or after October 7, 1998 you may receive a partial cancellation of your loan.

For further information, contact your school district or state department of education.

b. Teach in a federally designated teacher shortage area.

If you have a federal Perkins Loan and teach a subject such as science, math or a foreign language in an area in which there is a teacher shortage you may be able to have your loan cancelled.

For further information, contact your school district or state department of education. You can also get information on National Loan Forgiveness Programs available in your state by going to the web site for the American Federal of Teachers at **www.aft.org/edissues/teacherquality/recruit2.htm**.

c. Work in the health care field.

The National Health Service Corps offers loan forgiveness programs to doctors, nurse practitioners, physician assistants, midwives, dentists, dental hygienists, and others who are willing to work for two years in communities that have a shortage of health care professionals.

For further information, contact The National Health Service Corps at **www.nhsc.bhpr.hrsa.gov**.

d. Work in the child care field.

If you work full-time as a child-care provider in a facility that serves low-income families you may be eligible to have your Direct Loan and/or Federal Family Education (FEEL) loan forgiven. You can pick up a copy of the Child Care Provider Loan Forgiveness Application at your school's financial aid office.

e. Join the Peace Corps.

As a two-year volunteer in the Peace Corps, you may be able to have 30 percent of your Perkins student loan cancelled.

f. Join Americorps, Volunteers In Service to America or Teach for America.

You can earn educational awards of $4,725 for each year of service. This money can be used to pay off student loans or to pay future education costs.

For further information, contact -
Americorps at **www.americorps.org**
Volunteers in Service to America at **www.friendsofvista.org**
Teach for America at **www.teachforamerica.org**

g. Provide legal service.

Some law schools provide loan forgiveness and/or repayment programs for people willing to offer legal service in communities that have a shortage of lawyers. Currently there are over 50 schools that offer such programs.

To get a list of the law schools that have such a program go to web site for the National Association of Public Interest Law at **www.napil.org**.

h. Join the military.

The Military College Loan Repayment Program (CLRP) is an enlistment incentive offered by each branch of the service. For more information, go to **www.usmilitary.about.com/cs/joiningup/a/clrp_p.htm**

These are just some examples of loan repayment/forgiveness programs. To get a list of over 200 such programs, plus a list of employers who will help pay off student loans as part of the recruiting process, order The Loan Forgiveness Directory. You can get it from the Scholarship Resource Network Express by calling them on 518-580-1022. The cost is $22.00 plus shipping and handling.

10

Knock $150 off your homeowner insurance premium

A woman called an insurance agent and said, "I want to insure my house. Can you do it by phone?"

Insurance Agent: "I am sorry, madam, but I have to see it first".

Woman caller: "Then you had better get over here right away because the house is on fire".

Since no one wants to be in this position, it makes sense to have the right coverage in place if such a catastrophe should happen. So how do you get the appropriate coverage while keeping the premium down? There are several ways to accomplish this:

1. Understand commonly used homeowner insurance terms:

Additional Living Expense — Fire damage or other covered loss could increase your living costs if you are paying for a hotel, restaurant meals or laundromat, for example. In a standard homeowner policy, Loss of Use (Coverage D) will reimburse you for any additional living expenses you incur in an attempt to maintain a normal standard of living if your home is made uninhabitable by a covered peril. See Loss of Use.

Appurtenant Structure — In a property insurance policy, "appurtenant structures" are buildings on the same premises as the main, insured building. Appurtenant structures like garages or barns on your property are usually covered by homeowner insurance policy.

Arbitration Clause — In your property insurance contract, the arbitration clause provides a means for settlement when you and your insurer cannot agree on an acceptable claim payment. Appraisers representing each party select a neutral arbitrator; a judgment by any two of these three constitutes a binding settlement.

Bodily Injury (BI) — An important type of liability coverage, BI will pay legal damages awarded for injury or death for which you are held legally responsible.

Broad Theft Coverage — An endorsement to a dwelling policy that provides theft coverage for contents to a named insured, owner occupant.

Business Personal Property — In a homeowner policy, "business personal property" refers to items or "contents" owned by your business or company, such as a laptop you might bring home over the weekend. Coverage is usually limited to $2,500.

Coverage A — Called "Dwelling", this is the part of your home insurance policy that covers the home itself, frame, flooring and fixed objects. The amount of Coverage A is the cost to replace the structure of your home in the event of total loss. Other overages are usually based on a percentage of Coverage A.

Coverage B — This part of your policy covers "Other Structures" such as barns, sheds and garages.

Coverage C — "Personal Property" covers your belongings automatically for 50% of Coverage A.

Coverage D — "Loss of Use" takes into account expenses you will have if your home is uninhabitable because of a covered loss. It pays for temporary lodging and living expenses.

Coverage E — "Personal Liability" covers you for your legal responsibility for injury caused to others whether on or away from your own property.

Coverage F — "Medical Payments" pays medical costs if someone is injured on your property. A homeowner policy automatically covers $1,000. You can increase this coverage in $1,000 increments, up to $5,000. In order to collect more than this, the injured party must file for compensation under Coverage E.

Debris Removal Clause — While most property policies cover only direct damages caused by an insured peril, the "debris removal clause" covers the cost of removing debris produced by the peril's occurrence. For example, a hurricane sweeps through the state; a fallen tree will be removed only if it lands on your house. Debris Removal reimburses you for the cost of cleaning all the broken limbs and rubble.

Direct Loss — This is a damage or loss resulting as a direct consequence of an insured peril. For example, a computer lost in a fire is a direct loss; the data destroyed inside the computer is considered an indirect loss.

Direct Writer — When an insurance company offers its policies directly to consumers through its own employees, it's called a "direct writer." Electric Insurance Company is a direct writer.

Dwelling Forms — These are polices which cover a residence dwelling or building and the personal property inside. You can buy dwelling forms that vary by the degree of coverage they offer.

Earthquake Endorsement — Most homeowner policies exclude coverage for earthquake damage. People who are concerned about the risk of earthquakes can add an Earthquake Endorsement to cover damages.

Easement — An "easement" entitles its holder to specific interests, such as a right of way, in land owned by someone else.

Fire Resistive Construction — Building construction using fire-resistive materials in its roof, floors and exterior walls. See also Modified Fire-Resistive Construction.

Fire Wall — A wall designed to contain or seal off fires in a building.

Fireproof — Unfortunately, no one can make a building that cannot be damaged by fire. Today, insurers use the term "fire-resistive" to describe buildings that are practically resistant to most fire damage.

Flood — A temporary submersion, partial or complete, of ordinarily dry land by water or mud. Floods are typically caused by an overflow of waters, whether inland, tidal or from any accumulated runoff from any source. Flood is excluded under a typical homeowner insurance policy.

Flood Insurance — Policies sold to cover property owners from losses caused by floods or flooding, usually offered in conjunction with a government flood insurance plan.

Frame Construction — The most common form of housing construction, frame buildings are made primarily of wood frames and joists.

Guaranteed Replacement Cost — Guaranteed Replacement Cost coverage on homeowners' insurance means that your home will be repaired to its value at the time of loss, regardless of the amount of coverage carried.

For example, you estimate your home to have a full replacement value of $220,000. On your homeowner policy, you carry $220,000 coverage for the structure. If you have guaranteed replacement cost endorsement on your policy and the home is lost in a fire and the house costs $230,000 to rebuild, the policy will pay $230,000.

Increased Cost of Construction Insurance — Commonly added as an endorsement to homeowner policies, "increased cost of construction insurance" covers the additional costs of building repair or reconstruction when you rebuild with more expensive services, materials and techniques required by local ordinances.

Increased Hazard — Property insurance terms are tailored to the nature and use of the property as it exists when the policy is written. Should you introduce dangerous materials or activities into the property, like making fireworks, you will have added an increased hazard whose liabilities would not be covered by your policy.

Indirect Loss — Also known as consequential loss or damage, indirect loss results from, but is not caused directly by, a peril. If your business property burned down, for instance, the property itself is a direct loss, while the lost business revenues would be considered an indirect loss.

Inflation Guard Coverage — "Inflation Guard Coverage" provides automatic periodic increases on the building's property insurance, to reflect the effects of inflation on building replacement expenses.

Loss of Use Coverage — If your home becomes uninhabitable because of an insured peril, Loss of Use (Coverage D) provides compensation for additional living expenses incurred in an attempt to maintain a normal standard of living. Loss of Use is automatically included as 20% of the Replacement Cost amount you carry in Coverage A.

If your home were covered for $200,000, for example, Loss of Use coverage would provide up to $40,000 for additional living expenses. See Additional Living Expenses.

Loss Payable Clause — To protect lenders or lien holders, this clause extends coverage to parties with an insurable interest in your property, most often the institution holding your mortgage.

Masonry Noncombustible Construction — Refers to buildings constructed from noncombustible materials such as masonry walls of brick, cinder block, stone, tile, or other similar materials, and floors and roofs made of metal or other noncombustible materials.

Modified Fire-Resistive Construction — Building construction featuring exterior walls, floors and roofs made of fire-resistive materials such as masonry or metal.

Mortgage Clause — In policies covering mortgaged property, the "mortgage clause" protects the interests of the mortgagee for loss reimbursement and other rights of recovery, regardless of any acts or neglect by the insured.

Mortgagee — A lender or creditor, typically a bank, who holds the mortgage, and lends money secured by the value of the mortgaged property.

Mortgagor — Usually the homeowner who, as debtor, receives money in return for a property mortgage granted as a security for the loan.

Named Perils — Named Perils Insurance covers specific perils listed in a policy, as opposed to an "all-risk insurance" covering all losses except the ones excluded by name in the policy.

National Flood Insurance Program (NFIP) — A program backed by the United States government to provide flood insurance for fixed property. The NFIP writes policies directly and offers reimbursement to private carriers offering flood insurance.

Occupancy — Property insurance rates reflect the way the property is used. In general, "owner occupied" homeowner policies are less expensive than "non-owner occupied" policies.

Off Premises — Coverage you can obtain for personal property or "contents" which are away from the principle insured property. In most cases, the amount of this coverage is limited to a percentage of the property's total coverage.

Other Structures — Generally detached structures, such as a garage or tool shed, sharing property with the insured dwelling. Under a homeowner policy, "other structures" are automatically covered for 10% of the limit chosen for Coverage A.

Personal Property — Any of your property, such as furniture, clothing and consumer electronics, other than real estate property. Your homeowner policy covers the personal property of you and your family members.

Physical Damage — Actual damage to your property.

Replacement Cost — Coverage for the cost of replacing damaged property at the time of loss with that of similar kind and quality. If you carry replacement cost coverage and have a loss, the insurer pays for the cost of a new replacement, minus any policy deductible.

Residence Premises — Where you, the insured, live. In homeowner insurance, this includes the dwelling, grounds and other structures, or that part of any other building in which you live.

Riot — Violent activity by more than one person. The number of persons it takes to constitute a riot varies by state. Your policy may cover riots through extended coverage or direct reference.

Scheduled Personal Property — Personal belongings that are worth more than the limits of liability set in your policy can be insured by adding this endorsement.

Sinkhole Collapse — A special form of earth movement, covered by some homeowner insurance, referring to the sudden collapse or sinking of land into empty, underground spaces eroded by water. Most other forms of earth movement remain excluded from ordinary policies.

Smoke Damage — As opposed to fire damage caused by combustion, heat or burning, this is damage attributable to the smoke itself.

Stated Amount — In your policy, you may choose to cover certain items for a specific amount. In the event of loss, the insurer pays the stated amount regardless of the property's actual value. If, for example, you insured a painting for a stated amount of $15,000, in the event of theft you would recover the $15,000 (minus your deductible); even if the painting had accrued value after the policy had been signed.

2. Raise your deductible.

A deductible is the amount of money you have to pay toward a loss before your insurance company starts to pay. A typical deductible is $250. Most insurance companies recommend a deductible of at least $500. The higher your deductible, the more money you can save on your premiums. According to **www.insure.com,** these are some typical savings you might experience by raising your deductible:

Raising your deductible by:	Could lower your premium by:
$500	12%
$1,000	24%
$2,500	30%
$5,000	37%

3. Shop around.

It will take some time, but could save you a good sum of money. Ask your friends, check the Yellow Pages or call your state insurance department. This will give you an idea of price ranges and tell you which companies have the lowest prices.

You can also access insurance information for your state on the Internet at **http://www.naic.org/cis/**. States often make information available on typical rates charged by major insurers and many states provide the frequency of consumer complaints by company. Also check consumer guides, insurance agents, companies and online insurance quote services such **www.insure.com.**

But don't consider price alone. The insurer you select should offer a fair price and deliver the quality service you would expect if you needed assistance in filing a claim. So talk to a number of insurers to get a feeling for the type of service they give.

4. Buy your homeowner and auto insurance from the same company.

Some companies that sell homeowners, auto and liability coverage will give as much as 15 percent multi-policy discount if you buy two or more policies from them.

5. Make your home more disaster-resistant.

Ask your insurance agent or company representative what steps you can take to make your home more resistant to windstorms and other natural disasters. You may be able to save on your premiums by adding storm shutters, reinforcing your roof or buying stronger roofing materials. Older homes can be retrofitted to make them better able to withstand earthquakes. In addition, consider modernizing your heating, plumbing and electrical systems to reduce the risk of fire and water damage.

6. Insure the house, not the land.

The land under your house isn't at risk from theft, windstorm, fire and the other perils covered in your homeowner's policy. So don't include its value in deciding how much homeowners insurance to buy. If you do, you will pay a higher premium than you should.

7. Make your home less attractive to burglars.

You can usually get discounts of at least 5 percent each for a smoke detector, burglar alarm or dead-bolt locks. Some companies cut your premium by as much as 15 or 20 percent if you install a sophisticated sprinkler system and a fire and burglar alarm that rings at the police, fire or other monitoring stations. You may also get a discount for a security system that alerts an outside service. These systems are not cheap and not every system qualifies for a discount. Before you buy such a system, find out what kind your insurer recommends, how much the device would cost and how much you would save on premiums.

8. Explore group coverage.

If your employer administers a group insurance program, check to see if a homeowner's policy is available, and if it is a better deal than you can find elsewhere. In addition, professional, alumni and business groups often work out an insurance package with an insurance company, which includes a discount for association members. Ask your group's director if an insurer is offering a discount on homeowners insurance to you and your fellow graduates or colleagues.

9. Stay with an insurer that offers a good deal.

If you've kept your coverage with a company for several years, you may receive a special discount for being a long-term policyholder.

Some insurers will reduce their premiums by 5 percent if you stay with them for three to five years and by 10 percent if you remain a policyholder for six years or more.

10. Stop Smoking.

According to the Federal Emergency Management Agency, careless smoking is a leading cause of home fires. Some companies give a discount if no one in the house smokes.

11. Seek other discounts.

Companies offer several types of discounts, but they don't all offer the same discount or the same amount of discount in all states. That's why you should ask your agent or company representative about any discounts available to you. For example, since retired people stay at home more than working people, they are less likely to be burglarized and may spot fires sooner. Retired people also have more time for maintaining their homes. If you're at least 55 years old and retired, you may qualify for a discount of up to 10 percent at some companies. Other discounts to explore are fire-safe windows and earthquake retrofitting.

12. Review your policy annually.

You want to make sure your policy covers any major purchases or additions to your home. But you don't want to spend money for coverage you don't need. For example, if your five-year-old fur coat is no longer worth the $5,000 you paid for it, you'll want to reduce or cancel your floater (extra insurance for items whose full value is not covered by standard homeowners policies) and pocket the difference.

Typical questions homeowners ask when calling the Insurance Information Hotline:

Question #1: Are you covered for direct losses due to fire, lightning, tornadoes, windstorms, hail, explosions, smoke, vandalism and theft?

Answer: Yes. The HO-3 provides broad coverage for a large number of perils, including all those listed. There are some limits, however, on the amount of insurance you have.

Action: Check the dollar limits of insurance in your policy. Make sure you are comfortable with the amount of insurance you have for specific items. For example, the standard policy provides only $1,000 for theft of jewelry. If your jewelry is worth a lot more, you should purchase higher limits. You may wish to add a floater to your policy to cover specific possessions, such as expensive paintings or silverware. The floater will provide both higher limits and protect you from additional risks, not covered in your normal policy. Also, if you live on the Atlantic or Gulf coasts there may be some restrictions on your coverage for wind damage. Check this out with your agent.

Question #2: Your house is totally destroyed in a fire. You have bought $150,000 worth of insurance to cover the structure of your house. Will this be enough to rebuild your home?

Answer: If the cost of rebuilding your home were equal to or less than $150,000 you would have enough coverage. The HO-3 policy pays for structural damage on a replacement cost basis. If the cost of replacing your home is, say, $120,000, then that is all the insurance you need. On the other hand if the cost of rebuilding your home is $180,000, then you will be short $30,000. If you choose not to replace your home, you will receive the replacement cost of your home, less depreciation. This is called actual cash value.

Action: Make sure that the amount of insurance you have will cover the cost of rebuilding your house. You can find out what this cost is by talking to your insurance representative or builders in your area.

Do not use the price of your house as the basis for the amount of insurance you purchase. The market price of your house includes the value of the land on which the house is situated. In almost all cases, the land will be still there after a disaster, so you do not need to insure it. You only need to insure the structure.

Question #3: Are you covered for flood?

Answer: No.

Action: Flood insurance is provided by the federal government, under a program run by the Federal Insurance Administration. If you are in a flood prone area it may be wise to purchase flood insurance. In some parts of the country, homes can be damaged or destroyed by mudslides. This risk is also covered under flood policies. Contact your agent or company representative to get this insurance, or call 1-800-427-4661.

Question #4: A pipe bursts and water flows all over your floors. Are you covered?

Answer: Yes. The HO-3 covers you for accidental discharge of water from a plumbing system.

Action: Check your plumbing and heating systems once a year. While you are covered for damage, who needs the mess and hassle?

Question #5: Water seeps into your basement from the ground. Are you covered?

Answer: No. Water seepage is excluded under the HO-3. And if the water seepage is not due to a flood you will not be covered under a flood policy. Problems like seepage are viewed as maintenance issues and are not covered by insurance.

Action: You should see a contractor about waterproofing your basement.

Question #6: Are you covered for earthquake damage?

Answer: No.

Action: Earthquake coverage is sold as additional coverage to the homeowner's policy. To determine whether you should purchase this insurance, talk to your agent or company representative. In earthquake prone areas, the price of this insurance is relatively high. In other areas, it is relatively cheap.

Question #7: A neighbor slips on your sidewalk and threatens to take you to court for damages. Does your policy protect you?

Answer: Yes. The policy will pay for damages, if the accident is the result of your negligence. It will also pay for the legal costs of defending you against a claim. Also, the medical payments part of your homeowner's policy will cover medical expenses arising from an injury to a neighbor or guest.

Action: Check to see how much liability protection you have. The standard amount is $100,000. If you feel you need more, consider purchasing higher limits.

Question #8: During a storm, a tree falls and damages your roof. Are you covered?

Answer: Yes. You are covered for the damage to your roof. You are also covered for the removal of the tree, up to a $500 limit.

Action: Cut down dead or dying trees close to your house. Prune branches that are near your house. It's true that your insurance covers damage, but falling trees and branches can also injure your family.

Question #9: During a storm, a tree falls and does no damage to your property. Are you covered for the cost of removing the tree?

Answer: No. Your trees and shrubs are covered for losses due to risks like vandalism, theft and fire, but not wind damage.

Action: Decide if you need extra insurance for the trees, plants and shrubs on your property. You may be able to purchase extra insurance, which will not only cover the cost of removal of fallen trees, but will also cover the cost of replacing trees, and other plants. Talk to your insurance representative about the availability and cost of this extra insurance.

Question #10: During a storm, the power from the electric utility is lost. All the food in your refrigerator is spoiled and must be thrown out. Can you make a claim?

Answer: The general answer is no. However, there are a number of exceptions. In some states, food spoilage is covered under the homeowner's policy. In addition, if the power loss is due to a break in a power line on or close to your property, you may be covered.

Action: Check with your agent to determine whether you are covered for food spoilage in your state. If not, you can add food spoilage coverage to your policy for an additional premium.

Question #11: Your golf clubs are stolen from the trunk of your car. Can you recover?

Answer: Yes. The HO-3 covers your personal property while it is anywhere in the world. However, if your golf clubs are old, you will only get their current value. This normally will not be enough to purchase a new set.

Action: Consider purchasing a replacement cost endorsement for your personal property. This way you will get the full cost of replacing the golf clubs, less the applicable deductible.

Question #12: You have a powerboat with a 50 horsepower engine. If it is stolen, are you covered? What if there is a boating accident and you get sued? Are you covered?

Answer: If the boat is stolen from your residence, in most cases, you can recover only $1,000. If the boat is stolen elsewhere you are not covered. You are also not covered for liability arising from an accident with the boat. The homeowner's policy provides liability coverage for boats with engines less than 25 horsepower.

Action: See your insurance representative about getting extra coverage for your boat, including theft and liability. Ask about the Boat owner's policy.

11

Slice $100 off your monthly lunch bill

"Let's do lunch."

Studies show that the typical family spends $1632 per year in food away from home. A significant portion of the expenditure is for lunches. Just as you can cut the cost of food at home, there are ways to reduce the cost for lunch.

1. Brown bag it.

You could save $1200.00 per year. (Assume $5.00/day x 5 work days = $25.00 x 4 weeks/month x 12 = $1200.00). Pack your lunch the night before and leave a note for yourself so you don't forget to take it with you.

2. Keep some things at work for emergencies.

Peanut butter and crackers, instant soup and cereal are examples of quick ideas for those times when you don't take time to fix lunch.

3. Use a potluck system.

Team up with some coworkers and have each one bring an item for lunch and people can share. This can be a salad, dip, vegetable, etc. Maybe this can work one day per week.

12

7 ways to get free food at restaurants

Being frugal does not mean being deprived. There are times when you will want to eat out. When you do, however, you should look to take advantage of these money saving opportunities:

1. Use the Entertainment Book.

This entitles you to a 50 percent discount or allows you to buy one meal and get the second one free. The books, which include approximately 166 restaurants in North America, cost between $25 and $45. They also have discount coupons for fast food, oil changes, movies and a lot more. You can order a book by visiting **www.entertainment.com**.

2. Join iDinePrime.

This national program, which includes over 17,000 restaurants, gives you a 20% cash refund off your restaurant bill. Instead of a membership fee iDinePrime takes the first $49 you save. You can get further details and join by visiting them at **www.idine. com**.

3. Join www.restaurant.com.

Membership is free. You can purchase a gift certificate at a participating restaurant for $25 and redeem the certificate for $50 worth of food. An alternative is to purchase a gift certificate for $50 and redeem it for $100 worth of food.

4. Look for coupons online.

Go to **www.restaurantcoupons.net** and list your state and region. Indicate whether you are interested in fine dining, family casual, lunch specials, fast food or take out. You will get a list of member restaurants and coupons for each.

5. Get coupons at restaurants' website.

6. Ask for a senior citizen discount if you are 55 or over.

7. Identify restaurants that allow kids to eat free or at a discount.

www.kidseatfree.com has a state-by-state listing of restaurants at which kids can eat free. The list is not all-inclusive and is ever-changing, so you will want to check on the ones in your area.

Examples:

- o   At Chick Fil-A kids eat free.

- o   At Denny's kids eat free on Tuesday.

- o   At International House of Pancakes (IHOP) – One child per paying adult under 12 eats free from 3:00 p.m. – 11:00 p.m. Monday through Thursday.

o At Pizza Hut – On Tuesday night if you buy one medium or one large pizza your kids get two free personal pan pizzas.

13

7 more ways to save when you eat out

1. Order water with a lemon.

This is a great alternative to paying $1.79 and up for soda. You can even add sugar and presto – lemonade.

2. Skip dessert.

This is a terrific way to avoid adding needless dollars to your check and unwanted inches to your waistline.

3. Be an "Early-Bird".

In order to fill the tables, many restaurants offer an early bird special between 4:30 and 6:00. The portion is a little smaller but so is the check.

4. Do lunch instead of dinner.

A number of restaurants serve the same thing for lunch and for dinner. The only differences are that the lunch portion is smaller and the cost may be as much as $10 lower than dinner. As a bonus, if you have small kids and they are in day care, this can be a way to have a date with your spouse without having to pay for a babysitter.

5. Look for all-you can-eat buffets.

6. Identify restaurants that have special offers.

Some examples are:

Little Caesar has a large one topping pizza for $5.00 everyday.

Outback Steakhouse has an item called Joey Sirloin that is a nice size steak and it comes with a baked potato or sweet potato. The cost is $4.99 for children under 10. They will let an adult order and pay an additional $3.00 fee. I am waiting for them to run a special on the Blooming Onion.

7. Buy a cappuccino machine.

Instead of paying $3-$4 per cup, you can buy a 4 cup machine for as little as $40.00 and make your own. You will save over $700 per year. One place to purchase a machine is **www. goodmans.net**.

14

14 ways to save on entertainment

Studies show that a typical family spends over $1,800 per year in entertainment. There are a number of ways to cut costs while continuing to enjoy "The finer things in life."

1. Borrow movies from the public library.

This can save you a lot of money when you consider the following:

Movie tickets — $14/visit x 2 visits/month = $28/month x 12 = $336/year

Snacks at the movies — $5/visit x 2 visits/month = $10/month x 12 = $120/year

Video rentals — 3@ $9/weekend = 36/month x 12 = $432/year

Total savings: $888

2. Borrow puzzles and games for the kids from the public library.

3. Rent movies online.

Netflix will allow you to rent all the movies you want for $20 per month. An added benefit is that there is no late fee. Visit them at **www.netflix.com**.

4. Cancel cable.

If you are subscribing to extra cost cable TV channels and not watching them very much, if at all, consider canceling them. You can easily save $40 per month.

5. Cancel subscriptions to magazines that you never read.

6. Buy books at a discount.

If you like to read, you can purchase used books at half price at **www.half.com**.

7. Organize potluck dinners for friends and neighbors.

It is a great way to try different food and save money at the same time.

8. Take in a matinee.

If you insist on going to a movie make it a matinee since movie houses generally offer a discount. In addition, if you belong to the American Automobile Association (AAA) they will give you $3 discount coupons that are good at many theaters.

9. Go to $1.00 theaters.

Look for them in the yellow pages.

10. Form a baby-sitting cooperative.

Join other couples that you know and trust. This is can easily knock $20-30 off the cost of a well-deserved night out.

11. Attend Community College events.

Many community colleges have art shows, concerts, plays, etc. Admission is usually free, although sometimes they may charge a nominal fee. To find the community college nearest you, visit the American Association of Colleges at **www.aacc.nche.edu** and click on "Community College Finder."

12. Look for free or discounted events.

Contact your state's Department of Tourism, usually listed under the Department of Business and Economic Development. They will gladly send you a calendar of events along with coupons.

13. Attend high school or minor league sports rather than professional.

The level of play may not be as high but neither are the prices for admission, concessions and parking.

14. Look for travel discounts.

Visit **www.orbitz.com**. They offer discounts on airline tickets, hotels and car rentals. They also have weekend getaway specials.

15

17 ways to save on clothes

According to the U.S. Bureau of Labor Statistics, the average consumer spends approximately $1800 per year on purchasing and maintaining clothes. There are ways to save on both.

When shopping:

1. Avoid name brands.

2. If you must have brand names, buy them at factory outlets.

The savings can be as much as 40% off the retail price. If you call an outlet store many of them have salespeople who will tell you if they have a particular item that you may be looking for. If they don't have it, you can go to **www.outletbound.com**, type in the item you are looking for and they will give you a list of outlet stores that carry the item.

3. Avoid trendy clothes.

Instead, buy conservative clothes and dress them up with accessories. This gives you an opportunity to mix and match.

4. Buy at the right time.

After the holidays, at the of end of the season, buying winter clothes at the beginning of spring and summer clothes at beginning of fall are examples of the right times to buy.

5. Become friendly with a store salesperson.

He or she can let you know about upcoming sales and can hold items aside for you.

6. Shop online.

At sites like **www.hugestore.com** you can save as much as 25-30% off the retail price. At **www.onlyonsale.com** you can get savings of as much 50 – 70 % on brand name clothing for babies, kids and teens.

7. Buy clothes with slight defects.

8. Shop at bargain stores.

Stores such as Wal-Mart, Target, Kohl's and Ross offer great bargains on children's clothes.

9. Start a clothing Co-op.

Exchange clothing with family members, friends, and church members.

10. Go to thrift and consignment shops in upscale neighborhoods.

You will have to examine the clothes closely for defects but you can save as much as 40% off the retail price. A friend of ours paid $10 for a dress for her little girl. The retail price of the dress is $65.

On Dry-Cleaning:

1. Buy clothes that are washable.

2. Hang clothes up immediately.

3. Freshen up a suit with a fabric refresher.

Febreze Extra Strength is one that we have found to be effective.

4. Remove spills immediately.

5. Use Home dry-cleaning kits.

6. Look for discounts.

The dry cleaners we use will clean 3 garments for the price of 2 every day except Wednesday. So you can believe that any time we have dry cleaning we take it in on a day other than Wednesday.

16

7 ways to save on appliances

When you are shopping for appliances, you can think of two price tags. The first price tag covers the purchase price-think of that as a down payment. The second price tag covers the cost of operating the appliance. You will be paying on that price tag throughout the time you own it. There are a number of ways to save on both price tags.

1. Start your research early.

As Benjamin Franklin put it, "Necessity never made a good bargain". While your aging appliance is still working, begin looking for a replacement. Consider things such as features, prices and warranties.

2. Look for "Scratched and Dent".

Sometimes appliances get scratched and/or dented in the process of being delivered. When that happens, the retailer marks down the prices but sells it with the same warranty as a new one. My wife and I bought a 25 cubic foot refrigerator at 40 percent off the retail price because it had a scratch on the side. That did not matter to us because the scratch is not visible in the location we have the refrigerator.

3. Buy at the right time of year.

Various appliances offer the best sale at different times of the year. For example:

Spring
- o   Microwaves
- o   Room air conditioners

Right before Memorial Day
- o   Refrigerators

September
- o   Washers and dryers

4. Buy a floor model.

Even though it may have a few scuffmarks it will work fine, carries the same manufacturer warranty but offers a substantial saving off the retail price.

5. Search at www.salescircular.com.

They list over 120 products that are on sale each week. You can click on your state and see which retailer has the best deal on the product for which you are looking.

6. Look for the ENERGY STAR label.

The ENERGY STAR label is the government's seal of approval. It was created by the U.S. Department of Energy and the U.S. Environmental Protection Agency. These agencies set the criteria to help shoppers for large and small home appliance identify the most energy-efficient products on the market. ENERGY STAR-labeled appliances typically exceed federal efficiency standards by 13% to 20%. Based on that you can be assured you will save on energy use during the lifetime of the appliance. Let us look at some specific appliances:

Air-Source Heat Pumps

Look for the Energy Guide label that contains the SEER (Seasonal Energy Efficiency Ratio) and HSPF (Heating Seasonal Performance Factor) for heat pumps. The SEAR measures the energy efficiency during the cooling season and HSPF measures the efficiency during the heating season. The ENERGY STAR® minimum efficiency level is 12 SEER or higher.

Central Air Conditioners

Look for the Energy Guide label with a SEER (Seasonal Energy Efficiency Rating) for central air conditioners. The ENERGY STAR® minimum efficiency level is 12 SEER. ENERGY STAR® central air conditioners exceed federal standards by at least 20%.

Room Air Conditioners

Look for the Energy Guide label with an EER (Energy Efficiency Rating) for room air conditioners. The higher the EER, the more efficient the unit is. ENERGY STAR® units are among the most energy-efficient products.

Programmable Thermostats

For minimum ENERGY STAR® efficiency, thermostats should have at least two programs, four temperature settings each, a hold feature that allows you to temporarily override settings, and the ability to maintain room temperature within 2°F of desired temperature.

Refrigerators and Freezers

Look for the Energy Guide label that tells how much electricity, in kilowatt-hours (kWh), the refrigerator or freezer will use in one year. The smaller the number, the less energy it uses. ENERGY STAR® labeled units exceed federal standards by at least 20%.

Dishwashers

Look for the Energy Guide label that tells how much electricity, in kilowatt-hours (kWh), the dishwasher will use in one year. The smaller the number, the less energy it uses. ENERGY STAR® dishwashers exceed federal standards by at least 13%.

Clothes Washers

Look for the Energy Guide label that tells how much electricity, in kilowatt-hours (kWh), the clothes washer will use in one year. The smaller the number, the less energy it uses. ENERGY STAR® clothes washer uses less than 50% of the energy used by standard washers.

Water heaters

Look for the Energy Guide label that tells how much energy the water heater uses in one year. Also, look for the FHR (First Hour Rating) of the water heater, which measures the maximum hot water the heater will deliver in the first hour of use.

7. Skip the extended warranty.

Experts say that if something is going to go wrong it will usually do so during the time that the appliance is under the manufacturer warranty. Save the money you would pay for the extended warranty and use it to replace the item when it wears out.

17

8 ways to improve your credit score

As the saying goes, "Love may be blind, but creditors are not."

What is credit scoring?

Have you ever wondered how a creditor decides whether to grant you credit? For years, creditors have been using credit-scoring systems to determine if you would be a good risk for credit cards, auto loans and mortgages. More recently, some insurance companies have been using your credit score to determine if they are going to insure you, and if so, how much they will charge in premiums. Let us look at how credit scoring works in helping decide who gets credit and the cost of that credit:

Step 1: Information about you and your credit experiences is collected from your credit application and your credit report. Following is the kind of information creditors collect and evaluate:

o Have you paid your bills on time? Payment history typically is a significant factor. It is likely that your score will be affected negatively if you have paid bills late, had an account referred to collections, or declared bankruptcy.

o What is your outstanding debt? Many scoring models evaluate the amount of debt you have compared to your credit limits. If the amount you owe is close to your credit limit, it is likely to have a negative effect on your score.

o How long is your credit history? Generally, models consider the length of your credit track record. An insufficient credit history may have a negative effect on your score, but that can be offset by other factors, such as timely payments and low balances.

o Have you applied for new credit recently? Many scoring models consider whether you have applied for credit recently by looking at "inquiries" on your credit report when you apply for credit. If you have applied for too many new accounts recently, that may negatively affect your score. However, not all inquiries are counted. Inquiries by creditors who are monitoring your account or looking at credit reports to make "prescreened" credit offers are not counted.

o How many and what types of credit accounts do you have? Although it is generally good to have established credit accounts, too many credit card accounts may have a negative effect on your score. In addition, many models consider the type of credit accounts you have. For example, under some scoring models, loans from finance companies may negatively affect your credit score.

Note: Scoring models may be based on more than just information in your credit report. For example, the model may consider information from your credit application as well such as your job or occupation, length of employment, and whether you own a home.

Step 2: Using a statistical program, creditors compare this information to the credit performance of consumers with similar profiles. A credit scoring system awards points for each factor that helps predict who is most likely to repay a debt.

A total number of points -- a credit score -- helps predict how creditworthy you are, that is, how likely it is that you will repay a loan and make the payments when due.

How your credit score impacts how much you pay for a mortgage:

It affects the interest rate and – of course - the monthly payment. Using a model taken from the Fair Isaac Company, a leader in credit scoring, let us look at a hypothetical situation involving a 30-year fixed rate mortgage for $220,000:

Credit Score	APR	Monthly Payment	Total Interest
720-850	5.592 %	$1,262	$234,271
700-719	5.718 %	$1,279	$240,581
675-699	6.260 %	$1,356	$268,163
620-674	7.420 %	$1,526	$329.446
560-619	8.381 %	$1,673	$382,313
500-559	9.027 %	$1,774	$418,800

To find out how your specific credit score might impact your interest rate and mortgage payment go to **www.myfico.com/ creditcentral/loanrates.asp**

How to improve your credit score:

1. Review your credit report for errors.

You can get a copy by contacting the three major credit-reporting agencies:

Equifax: **www.equifax.com** or call 1-800-685-1111

Experian: **www.experian.com** or call 1-888-397-3742

Trans Union: **www.transunion.com** or call 1-800- 916-8800

The cost is approximately $9.00.

Report all errors to the credit reporting agencies right away.

2. Pay your bills on time.

3. Pay down outstanding balances.

Pay as much as you can on every account, and never pay less than the minimum.

4. Stay below the limit.

Your credit score also considers how much credit is available to you. If you regularly charge close to the maximum on your charge card, you will hurt your credit score.

5. Group your inquiries.

When you shop for a loan, each lender will check your credit history. Every "inquiry" is listed on your credit report. The credit scoring system sees too many inquiries as a sign of risk. Avoid this problem by comparison shopping within a short time period. If you make several inquiries about one type of loan, say a car loan, within one month, FICO counts this as only one inquiry. By the way, when you check your own report (make an "inquiry") you do not harm your score.

6. Have fewer accounts.

If you apply for store credit to get a special offer or discount, you may harm your score, even if you don't use the store account often. Many credit card companies send pre-approved offers for you to get a credit card and transfer outstanding balances to the new card at "0" annual percentage rate for 6 months. Opening a new account and transferring your existing balances to the new account will not improve your score.

7. Avoid taking on any new debt.

8. Allow some time to improve your score significantly.

Late payments can lower your score quickly, and it will take time to recover. Establish and maintain the habit of paying on time. The credit scoring formulas give more weight to the recent positive history. Give older poor performance time to fade away.

18

Avoid overpaying when buying a house

Housebroken: What you are after buying a house.

—Anonymous

Before looking at houses:

1. Recognize that it is important to go slowly.

This is probably the biggest purchase you are going to make, so you need to time to research things like the neighborhood, prices for which houses are selling, the quality of the schools and how long it will take you to commute to and from work during rush hour.

2. Determine your credit score.

Since your credit score has a large impact on the interest rate you will pay it is important to have as high a credit score as possible. See Chapter 17 for a full discussion on the definition of credit scoring, how a credit score is determined, how to get a copy of your credit report and how to improve your credit score.

3. Decide how much you can afford as a down payment.

4. Decide how much you can afford to pay each month.

For assistance, go to **www.ginniemae.gov**. Click on "Path to Homeownership". Click on "Affordability Calculator".

5. Select a buyer's agent.

In a typical situation, you will deal with a real estate agent who is contractually obligated to represent the seller's interest. As such, his/her job is to get you to buy the house at a price and on terms that are most favorable to the seller. You need someone who can help you purchase the house at a price and on terms that are most favorable to you. In addition to helping you get pre-approved for a mortgage a buyer agent will:

o   Give valuable information about the general housing market.
o   Give you information about neighborhoods and house values.
o   Point out defects in a house.
o   Help you find a home inspector.
o   Help you negotiate the best price and terms.

Since a buyer agent's fee is generally included in the commission you would pay anyway, using one generally does not cost you anything extra. The key is to decide early in the process if you are going to use a buyer agent. If you wait until you have toured open houses, called real estate agents for information about listings, toured one of more homes with a salesperson or broker or provided your email address over the internet to receive listing updates, it could cause problems in working with a buyer's agent.

Finding a buyer's agent

a. Your best bet is to find and work with an Exclusive Buyer Agent (EBA). An EBA only represents buyers, never takes listings or represents sellers and has his/her real estate license with a company that only represents buyers. This gives you the best opportunity to be properly represented, regardless of which property you are interested in buying.

To find an Exclusive Buyer Agent in your area go to the web site for the National Association of Exclusive Buyer Agents at **www. naeba.com** and click on "Find Your Best Agent". You can also call them on 1-800-986-2322.

b. If there are no Exclusive Buyer Agents in your area, your next best choice is an Accredited Buyer Representative (ABR). To find an ABR in your area go to the web site for the Real Estate Buyer's Agent Council at **www.rebac.net** and click on "Find a Buyer Agent". You can also call them on 1-800-648-6224.

c. Develop a list of at least three potential buyer agents, either EBAs or ABRs or a combination of the two. Some questions to ask:

- How long have you been representing buyers?
- What is your fee and who pays it?
- Do I sign a contract with you? If so, for what duration? What is the cancellation process? (Note: Agents may want you to sign a written agreement for 90 days. If you are uncomfortable with that time frame ask for a maximum of 30 days. At the end of 30 days if you are not satisfied with the agent's performance you can find another agent. If you are satisfied you can renew the agreement for another 30 to 60 days.

A written buyer agreement is a legally binding document. So, you may want to have an attorney review it. Beware of agents who don't use written agreements. The advantage of a written agreement is that it puts all terms, including the duration of the relationship and the agent's fee in writing where you can review them and avoid any surprises later).

6. Get pre-approved rather than pre-qualified.

o Pre-qualification is an estimate of what you can afford. The lender collects basic information regarding your income, monthly debts, credit history and assets, and then uses this information to calculate an estimated mortgage amount for which you might qualify.

o Pre-approval uses basic information as well as electronic credit reporting. After having collected and analyzed the data, the lender makes a written commitment to making the loan for a specific amount provided that you make a purchase within a specified period of time.

Benefits of getting pre-approved:

o The pre-approval letter let's the seller know you are a serious buyer.

o Since sellers are more apt to negotiate with someone who already has a mortgage approval in hand, you will have a greatly improved negotiating position.

o As a pre-approved buyer you can also close on a property more quickly - another major consideration for a motivated seller.

Questions to ask before making a purchase offer:

a) Why is the house being sold?

It is important to know this because it helps you determine the seller's level of desperation. If the seller has lost his/her job, has been relocated by his/her employer, is going through a divorce or if it is an estate sale he/she may be motivated to sell quickly. This can lead to your being able to negotiate a lower price and/or more favorable terms.

b) How much did the seller pay for the house?

Here, you are trying to determine how much room the seller may have to negotiate. If he has been in the house for a few years there is a good chance there is a fair amount of equity and you may be able to negotiate a price lower than what the seller is asking. This information is available at the city/county office where deeds are filed. Your buyer's agent can get this information for you.

c) What is the neighborhood like?

The time to find out about problems such as noise and traffic is not after you have gone to settlement. Talk with the neighbors. Tell them you are thinking of buying the house next door/across the street. Ask them for their assessment of the neighborhood. If you have kids, find out if there are other kids in the neighborhood?

It is always a good idea to drive, walk or bike through the neighborhood at different times of the day/ night and days of the week to get a "feel" for the environment.

d) How old is the roof?

This is potentially a large expense soon after you take ownership. The seller may have to disclose the age on the property-condition form, but if the roof was there before he purchased the house, he can truthfully say he doesn't know. Make sure your home inspector examines the roof closely.

e) How old is the furnace?

This is another potential for a large expense. Look for the service record on the side of the furnace. That will not only tell you when it was installed, but when it has been cleaned. You will want to make a thorough inspection first. If it looks okay, have your home inspector do an even more thorough examination.

g) Has this property ever been rented?

Rentals obviously take far more abuse than owner-occupied houses. If the property was used as a rental at some time, pay special attention to it's overall condition.

h) What are the test scores of the local schools?

This is critical, even if you don't have children. Since the average homeowner moves every 7 years, you have to think of the potential resale of the property. The quality of the schools will greatly enhance the resale value. You can contact the school district to get information on test scores.

7. Ignore the asking price.

Many times houses sell below the asking price, so do not get locked into thinking that you have to meet or even exceed that price.

8. Get a CMA.

No, it is not a Country Music Award. It is a Certified Market Analysis. This lets you know the prices for which houses in the neighborhood are listed and the prices for which house have sold recently. Your buyer agent can get this for you.

9. Make your offer attractive to the seller.

When the supply of good-conditioned homes for sale is limited and the demand is strong, you can expect to face multiple offer situations. So you need to make an offer that is not ridiculously over the market value but is attractive to the seller: Some ways to do that:

- o Offer the highest price you can.
- o Attach a copy of you pre-approval letter to your offer.
- o Make as large a down payment as you can and provide documentation showing the source of your down payment (e.g., a bank statement).
- o If your current home is being sold and you have a contract, include this information with your offer.
- o Avoid unnecessary contingencies, such as, "Subject to a final inspection to determine if my bedroom dresser will fit into the master bedroom".

10. Include a contingency that allows you get a certified home inspection.

The contingency should include what happens if you find something that is not acceptable. Do you fix it, does seller fix it or do you cancel contract offer and receive a full refund of your deposit?

11. Hire a competent home inspector.

It is critically important to have someone who is knowledgeable about construction, electrical, plumbing, soil grading, etc. to go over the house thoroughly before you consummate the deal. If there is a serious problem you want to know about it.

This gives you the opportunity to ask the seller to make necessary repairs, reduce the sale price so you can make the repairs or to cancel the offer to purchase with a full refund of your deposit. As for finding an inspector – ask your buyer broker for names. You might also ask people who have bought a house recently. Having gotten the names you should interview at least two home inspectors. Issues to explore during the interviews include:

a. Qualifications. How long has he/she been inspecting homes? This is no time for on-the-job training. You want experience.

b. Scope. How thorough is the inspection? As a minimum you want the inspection to include the roof, furnace, compressor, hot water heater, sump pump, appliances, plumbing, electrical, and the grading of the property. (Water should run away from-not towards-the house.)

c. Sample report. Ask to see what a final report looks like. Is it clear? Complete? Understandable? Is it thorough enough for you to feel comfortable proceeding with the purchase of the house?

d. References. Ask for the names and telephone numbers of several homeowners who have used his/ her services during the past twelve months. Call at least three people and ask them if they discovered anything that the inspector missed.

e. Memberships. Membership in an organization such as the National Association of Home Inspectors may mean that the inspector is more current on the latest industry practices.

f. Errors and omissions. No matter how good an inspector is, he/she can miss something. Find out what happens in that case. Does the inspector guarantee the report? As a minimum, you should expect to have the cost of the inspection refunded.

12. Ask for incentives if it is a new house.

In order to attract buyers, many times the builder will pay money that you can use towards the closing costs or to pay down the mortgage rates for the first few years. If the builder does not offer, ask.

13. Never buy the best house in the neighborhood.

The value of lower-priced houses in the neighborhood tends to pull down the values of the more expensive houses. On the other hand, more expensive houses pull up the value of lower priced houses.

14. Ask the "All-Important" Question.

The "All-Important" questions is, "Could I sell this house within 6 months and make a profit"? According to appraisers, every neighborhood has a "Value Range". Suppose that range is between $250,000 and $275,000. If you are considering paying $275,000 for a house in that neighborhood that is probably too much.

On the other hand, if you are considering paying $250,000 when comparable houses have been selling for $275,000 there is a good chance the answer to the "All-Important" question is "Yes".

19

9 ways to save when seeking a mortgage

Before you begin looking:

1. Determine your credit score.

Since your credit score has a large impact on the interest rate you receive, you want to have the highest credit score possible. See Chapter 17 for a full discussion on the definition of credit scoring, how a credit score is determined, how to get a copy of your credit report and how to improve your credit score.

2. Determine how much you can afford as a down payment.

3. Determine how much you can afford to pay each month.

See the affordability calculator at **www.ginniemae.gov**.

4. Understand commonly used mortgage terms:

Abstract of Title — A historical summary of all the recorded transactions that affect the title to the property. An attorney or a title company will review an abstract of title to determine if there are any problems affecting the title to the property. All such problems must be cleared before the buyer can be issued a clear and insurable title.

Acceleration Clause — A clause in your mortgage that allows the lender to demand payment of the outstanding loan balance for various reasons. The most common reasons for accelerating a loan are if the borrower defaults on the loan or transfers title to another individual without informing the lender.

Accelerated Mortgage Plan — A plan that increases the amount or frequency of loan payments so as to pay down the principal owed on a property before the standard term expires. If done correctly, an accelerated mortgage plan can save thousands of dollars in interest and provide full ownership of a property in less time than would be required if only the minimum required payment were made throughout the life of the loan.

Adjustable Rate Mortgage (ARM, also called Variable Rate Mortgage) — A mortgage with an interest rate that is adjusted periodically to reflect changes in market conditions. Your mortgage payments are adjusted up or down as the interest rate changes.

Adjustment Period — This is the length of time for which the interest rate is fixed on an Adjustable Rate Mortgage. Therefore if the adjustment period is six months, then the interest rate will remain fixed for six months, after which time it will adjust.

Agreement of Sale — A written signed agreement between the seller and the purchaser in which the purchaser agrees to buy certain real estate and the seller agrees to sell upon terms of the agreement. Also known as contract of purchase, purchase agreement and offer and acceptance.

Amortization — Payment of a debt in regular, periodic installments of principal and interest as opposed to interest only payments.

Annual Percentage Rate (APR) — An interest rate reflecting the actual finance cost of a mortgage as a yearly rate. Because APR includes points and other costs, it's usually higher than the advertised rate. The APR allows you to compare different mortgages based on actual annual costs.

Appraisal — An estimate of the value of a home, made by a professional appraiser. The maximum amount of the mortgage is usually based on a percentage of the appraisal.

Appreciation — The increase in the value of a property due to changes in market conditions, inflation, or other causes.

Assumable Mortgage — A mortgage loan that allows a new homebuyer to take over the obligation of making loan payments with no change in the terms of the loan. Assumable loans do not have a due-on-sale clause. The lender has to be notified and agree to the assumption. The lender may require the buyer to qualify for the loan and may charge an assumption fee. The seller should obtain a written release from the lender stating clearly that he/she is no longer liable to make mortgage payments.

Balloon Mortgage — A mortgage loan that requires the remaining principal balance be paid at a specific point in time. For example, a loan may be amortized as if it would be paid over a thirty- year period, but requires that at the end of the tenth year the entire remaining balance must be paid.

Binder — A title insurance binder is the written commitment of a title insurance company to insure title to the property subject to the conditions and exclusions shown in the binder.

Bi-Weekly Mortgage — A mortgage in which you make payments every two weeks instead of once a month. The basic result is that instead of making twelve monthly payments during the year, you make thirteen.

The extra payment reduces the principal, substantially reducing the time it takes to pay off a thirty-year mortgage.

Broker — As it relates to the real estate, a mortgage broker does not lend money, but acts as an agent between the borrower and the lender to secure financing. A broker can often be a more effective means for securing a loan because he or she is able to "shop" for the best rate and term available from several different lending sources at one time, something that would take a borrower much longer to do on his or her own. Brokers earn a profit for this service usually expressed as "points" on a loan.

Buy down — Money advanced by an individual (builder, seller, etc.) to reduce the monthly payments for a home mortgage either during the entire term or for an initial period of years. A "2-1" Buy down can be used to qualify a borrower who otherwise may not qualify for a loan by reducing the interest rate on the first two years of payments, thereby making the mortgage more affordable.

Buyer's Agent — A real estate agent hired by a buyer to locate a property for purchase. The broker represents the buyer and negotiates with the seller's broker for the best possible deal for the buyer. Buyer's Agents do not charge for their services; they split the commission with the seller's Listing Agent instead as compensation for their assistance in selling the property.

Buyers' Market — Market conditions that favor buyers i.e. there are more sellers than buyers in the market. As a result buyers have ample choice of properties and may negotiate lower prices. Buyers markets may be caused by an economic slump or overbuilding.

Cap — Adjustable Rate Mortgages have fluctuating interest rates, but those fluctuations are usually limited to a certain amount.

Those limitations may apply to how much the loan may adjust over a six-month period, an annual period, and over the life of the loan, and are referred to as "caps." Some ARMs, although they may have a life cap, allow the interest rate to fluctuate freely, but require a certain minimum payment that can change once a year. There is a limit on how much that payment can change each year, and that limit is also referred to as a cap.

Cash-Out Refinance — When a borrower refinances his mortgage at a higher amount than the current loan balance with the intention of pulling out money for personal use, it is referred to as "cash out refinance".

Certificate of Eligibility — The document issued by the Veterans Administration to those that qualify for a VA loan which may be used to buy a house with 0 down. Certificates of eligibility may be obtained by sending the form DD-214 to the local VA office along with VA form 1880.

Certificate of Title — An opinion rendered by an attorney as to the status of title to a property, according to the public records. This certificate does not provide the same level of protection as title insurance.

Closing — The consummation of a real estate transaction. The closing includes the delivery of a deed, financial adjustments, the signing of notes, and the disbursement of funds necessary to complete the sale and loan transaction.

Closing Costs (Settlement Costs) — All the charges associated with getting your mortgage, including the origination fee, discount points, appraisal fee, title search and insurance, survey, taxes, deed recording fee, charges for credit reports and other costs. Costs of closing usually add up to 3 to 6 percent of the mortgage amount.

Collateral — Property pledged as security for a debt, such as the real estate pledged as security for a mortgage.

Commitment Letter — A formal offer by a lender stating the terms under which they agree to loan money to a homebuyer.

Comparable Sales ("Comps") — Recent sales of similar properties in nearby areas and used to help determine the market value of a property.

Conforming Loan — Conventional home mortgages eligible for sale and delivery to either the Federal National Mortgage Association (FNMA) or the Federal Home Loan Mortgage Corporation (FHLMC). These agencies generally purchase first mortgages up to loan amounts mandated by Congressional directive. This amount is currently $300,700.00 or less.

Contingency — A condition that must be met before a contract is legally binding.

Contract — An agreement between competent parties to do or not do certain things for consideration.

Contract Sale or Deed — A real estate installment selling arrangement where the buyer may occupy the property but the seller retains the title until the agreed upon sales price has been paid. Also known as an installment land contract.

Conventional Mortgage — A mortgage not obtained under a government insured program (such as FHA or VA). A conventional loan may be conforming or non-conforming.

Convertible ARM (Adjustable Rate Mortgage) — An adjustable-rate mortgage that allows the borrower to change the ARM to a fixed-rate mortgage within a specific time.

Conveyance — The transfer of title of real property from one party to another.

Credit Rating — Borrowers are rated by lenders according to the borrower's credit-worthiness or risk profile. Credit ratings are expressed as letter grades such as A-, B, or C+. These ratings are based on various factors such as a borrower's payment history, available credit, and derogatory information, among others. There is no exact science to rating a borrower's credit, and different lenders may assign different grades to the same borrower. A FICO Score is used as a measure of creditworthiness, and is represented as a numerical score assigned by each of the three primary credit-reporting agencies.

Credit Report — A report detailing an individual's credit history.

Debt-to-Income Ratio (DIR) — Used as one of the primary considerations for a loan approval, a borrower's debt-to-income ratio is expressed as a percentage of the total amount of monthly payment obligations for secured and unsecured debt compared to total gross monthly income. The ratio of debt to income is 50% or less in order to qualify for a loan in most circumstances.

Deed — A written document by which title to real property is transferred from one owner to another. The deed should contain an accurate description of the property being conveyed, should be signed and witnessed according to the laws of the State where the property is located, and should be delivered to the buyer at closing.

Deed of Trust — An instrument used in many states (including California) in place of a mortgage. Property is transferred to a trustee by the borrower (trustor), in favor of the lender (beneficiary) and reconveyed upon payment in full.

Deposit — A sum of money given to bind a sale of real estate. Also known as earnest money.

Documentary Tax Stamp — Stamp affixed to a deed showing the amount of transfer tax.

Down Payment — The part of the purchase price of a property that the buyer pays in cash and does not finance with a mortgage.

Earnest Money — A portion of the down payment delivered with a purchase offer by the purchaser of real estate to the seller or an escrow agency by the purchaser of real estate with a purchase offer as evidence of good faith. Also known as a deposit.

Equity — The ownership interest; i.e. portion of a property's value over and above the liens against it.

Escrow Account — Once you close your purchase transaction, you may have an escrow account or impound account with your lender. This means the amount you pay each month includes an amount above what would be required if you were only paying your principal and interest. The extra money is held in your impound account (escrow account) for the payment of items like property taxes and homeowner's insurance when they come due. The lender pays them with your money instead of you paying them yourself.

Escrow Analysis — Once each year your lender will perform an "escrow analysis" to make sure they are collecting the correct amount of money for the anticipated expenditures.

Escrow Disbursements — The use of escrow funds to pay real estate taxes, hazard insurance, mortgage insurance, and other property expenses as they become due.

FSBO ("Fisboe") — Term meaning "For Sale By Owner". A property for sale that is not listed with a real estate broker.

Fair Market Value — The highest price that a buyer, willing but not compelled to buy, would pay, and the lowest a seller, willing but not compelled to sell, would accept.

Farmers Home Administration (FmHA) — An agency within the U.S. Department of Agriculture that administers assistance programs for purchasers of homes and farms in small towns and rural areas.

Federal Home Loan Mortgage Corporation — FHLMC (FREDDIE MAC) - Popularly known as Freddie Mac. A quasi-governmental agency that purchases conventional mortgages in the secondary mortgage market from insured depository institutions and HUD-approved mortgage bankers. It sells participation sales certificates secured by pools of conventional mortgage loans, their principal, and interest guaranteed by the federal government through the FHLMC. It also sells Government National Mortgage Association bonds to raise funds to finance the purchase of mortgages.

Federal Housing Administration (FHA) — An agency of the U.S. Department of Housing and Urban Development (HUD). Its main activity is the insuring of residential mortgage loans made by private lenders. The FHA sets standards for construction and underwriting but does not lend money or plan or construct housing.

Federal National Mortgage Association — FNMA (FANNIE MAE) - A taxpaying corporation created by Congress to support the secondary mortgage market. It purchases and sells residential mortgages insured by the Federal Housing Administration (FHA) or guaranteed by the Veterans Administration (VA) as well as conventional home mortgages.

183

FHA Mortgage — A mortgage that is insured by the Federal Housing Administration (FHA). Along with VA loans, an FHA loan will often be referred to as a government loan.

First Mortgage — A real estate loan that has priority over any subsequently recorded mortgages.

Fixture — Personal property that becomes real property when attached in a permanent manner to real estate.

Fixed Rate Mortgage — A mortgage with an interest rate that stays the same (fixed) for the life of the mortgage.

Interest — The sum of finance costs you pay for borrowing money. Interest income pays the lender's costs of doing business.

Marketable title — A title that is free of clouds and disputed interests.

Mortgage Note — A written promise to pay a sum of money at a stated interest rate during a specified term. The note contains a complete description of the conditions under which the loan is to be repaid and when it is due.

Mortgagor — The borrower in a mortgage transaction who pledges property as security for a debt.

Negative Amortization — Some adjustable rate mortgages allow the interest rate to fluctuate independently of a required minimum payment. If a borrower makes only the minimum payment it may not cover all of the interest that would normally be due at the current interest rate. In essence, the borrower is deferring the interest payment, which is why this is called "deferred interest." The deferred interest is added to the balance of the loan and the loan balance grows larger instead of smaller, which is called negative amortization.

Non-Conforming Loan — Conventional home mortgages not eligible for sale and delivery to either FNMA or FHLMC because of various reasons, including loan amount, loan characteristics or underwriting guidelines.

Note — A legal document that obligates a borrower to repay a mortgage loan at a stated interest rate during a specified period of time.

Origination Fee — The fee charged by a lender to prepare all the documents associated with your mortgage.

Percentage Point — One percent of the loan amount or a measure of the interest rate.

PITI (Principal, Interest, Taxes, and Insurance) — The most common components of a monthly mortgage payment.

Points — Fees paid to lenders. 1 Point = 1% of the loan amount. For example: on a $100,000 loan 1 Point is $1,000. Points may be further classified into Origination points or loan "Discount" Points.

Pre-Approval — A process that uses basic information as well as electronic credit reporting. After having collected an analyzed the data the lender makes a written commitment to making the loan for a specific amount provided that the applicant makes a purchase within a specified period of time. Most lenders can help you through the pre-approval process. In most cases, there is no charge for this service. Obtaining a pre-approved mortgage is essential in a "sellers' market" or where supply is limited.

Preliminary Title Report — The results of a title search by a title company prior to issuing a title binder or commitment to insure clear title.

Prepaid Interest — Prepaid interest is the interest charged to borrowers at closing to pay for the cost of borrowing for a balance of the month. Example: A loan closes on the 19th of the month and the first payment is due on the 1st of the following month, the lender will charge 12 days of prepaid interest.

Pre-paids — Expenses such as taxes, insurance and assessments which are paid in advance of their due date and which must be paid by the buyer on a prorated basis at closing.

Prepayment — Any amount paid to reduce the principal balance of a loan before the due date. Examples are: payment in full on a mortgage that may result from a sale of the property, the owner's decision to pay off the loan in full, or a foreclosure. In each case, prepayment means payment occurs before the loan has due to be paid off.

Prepayment Penalty — A fee that may be charged to a borrower who pays off a loan before it is due.

Pre-Qualification — This usually refers to the loan officer's written opinion of the ability of a borrower to qualify for a home loan, after the loan officer has made inquiries about debt, income, and savings. The information provided to the loan officer may have been presented verbally or in the form of documentation, and the loan officer may not have reviewed a credit report on the borrower.

Prime Rate — The interest rate that banks charge to their preferred customers. Changes in the prime rate are widely publicized in the news media and are used as the indexes in some adjustable rate mortgages, especially home equity lines of credit. Changes in the prime rate do not directly affect other types of mortgages, but the same factors that influence the prime rate also affect the interest rates of mortgage loans.

Principal Balance — The remaining balance due on a debt, exclusive of accrued interest.

Private Mortgage Insurance (PMI) — An insurance policy the borrower buys to protect the lender from non-payment of the loan. PMI policies are usually required if you make a down payment that is below 20% of the appraised value of the home.

Purchase Contract (Agreement/Offer) — An agreement between a buyer and seller of real property, setting forth the price and terms of the sale. Also known as a sales contract.

Qualifying Ratios — Calculations that are used in determining whether a borrower can qualify for a mortgage. There are two ratios. The "top" or "front" ratio is a calculation of the borrower's monthly housing costs (principle, taxes, insurance, mortgage insurance, and homeowner's association fees) as a percentage of monthly income. The "back" or "bottom" ratio includes housing costs as well as all other monthly debt.

Refinancing — Repayment of a debt from the proceeds of a new loan using the same property as security.

Rollover Loan — A loan that is amortized over a long period of time (e.g. 30 years) but the interest rate is fixed for a short period (e.g. 5 years). The loan may be extended or rolled over, at the end of the shorter term, based on the terms of the loan.

Second Mortgage — A subordinated lien, created by a mortgage loan, over the amount of a first mortgage. Second mortgages generally carry a higher rate than a first mortgage since they represent a higher risk for lender.

Title — The legal evidence of ownership rights to real property.

Title Insurance Policy — A contract in which an insurer, usually a title insurance company, agrees to pay the insured party a specific amount for any loss caused by defects of title on real estate in which the insured has an interest as purchaser, mortgagee, or otherwise.

Title Report — A document indicating the current state of title. The report includes information on the current ownership, outstanding deeds of trust or mortgages, liens, easements, covenants, restrictions, and any defects.

Title Search — An examination of public records to disclose the past and current facts regarding the ownership of a given piece of real estate.

Transfer of Ownership — Any means by which the ownership of a property changes hands. Lenders consider all of the following situations to be a transfer of ownership: the purchase of a property "subject to" the mortgage, the assumption of the mortgage debt by the property purchaser, and any exchange of possession of the property under a land sales contract or any other land trust device.

Transfer Tax — Tax paid to the city, county, state or other government entity upon sale of a property.

Truth-in-Lending Act — A Federal law requiring full disclosure of credit terms using a standard format. This is intended to facilitate comparisons between the lending terms and financial institutions.

Two-Step Mortgage — An adjustable-rate mortgage (ARM) that has one interest rate for the first five or seven years of its mortgage term and a different interest rate for the remainder of the amortization term.

Underwriting — Analysis of risk and setting of an appropriate rate and terms for a mortgage on a given property for given borrowers.

Unencumbered Property — Real estate with free and clear title.

VA Mortgage — A mortgage that is guaranteed by the Department of Veterans Affairs (VA).

Variable Rate Mortgage — Same as Adjustable Rate Mortgage.

Verification of Deposit (VOD) — A document signed by the borrower's bank or other financial institution verifying the account balance and history.

Verification of Employment (VOE) — A document signed by the borrower's employer verifying his/her starting date, job title, salary and probability of continued employment.

Veterans Affairs (VA) — An agency of the federal government that guarantees residential mortgages made to eligible veterans of the military services. The guarantee protects the lender against loss and thus encourages lenders to make mortgages to veterans.

Wrap-Around Mortgage — A loan arrangement whereby the existing loan is retained and a new loan is added to the property. Example: The seller sells his/her property for $200,000. The buyer puts $80,000 down. The seller has an existing loan balance of $100,000 for a remaining period of 25 years at an interest rate of 6%. The seller then makes a wraparound mortgage to the buyer, (where the seller acts as a lender) for $120,000 at 8%. The seller has to continue making payments on his old loan. The buyer has to pay the seller on the new loan. The buyer may at a later date refinance the property and close both loans.

5. Shop

Since mortgages are available from several types of lenders, you will want to get quotes from several lenders before making your final decision. Sources for quotes include:

- o   Thrift institutions.

- o   Commercial banks.

- o   Mortgage companies.

- o   Credit unions – Credit unions are a good source because unlike banks they are not profit-driven. They pass any income over the required reserves on to the members in the form of lower rates, lower fees and services. To find a credit union that is right for you and for which you are eligible to join, go **www.ncua.org** and click on "Credit Union Data".

- o   Online at sites such as **www.bankrate.com**, **www. lowermybills.com** and **www.lendingtree.com**.

Use the following worksheet to record information that you gather:

Mortgage Shopping Worksheet

	Mortgage 1	Mortgage 2
Name of Lender		
Name of Contact		
Date of Contact		
Mortgage Amount		
A. Information about the loan		
Type of Loan (Fixed rate, variable rate, conventional, other)		
Minimum down payment requirement		
Loan term (length of loan)		
Contract interest rate		
Annual Percentage Rate (APR)		
Points (may be called discount points)		
Monthly PMI payments		
How long must you keep PMI?		
Estimated monthly escrow for taxes and insurance		
Estimated monthly payment (include PITI and PMI)		
B. Fees associated with getting the loan		
Application of loan processing fee		
Origination or underwriting fee		
Lender fee or funding fee		
Appraisal fee		
Attorney fees		
Document preparation and recording fees		

Broker fees (may be quoted as points, origination fees, or interest rate add-on)		
Credit report fee		
Total fees		
C. Other costs due at settlement		
Title Search/Title Insurance		
Estimated prepaid amounts for interest, taxes, hazard insurance, payments for escrow		
State and local taxes, stamp taxes, transfer taxes		
Flood determination		
Prepaid PMI		
Surveys and home inspections		
D. Total (B+C)		
E. Miscellaneous questions		
Can any of the fees of costs be waived?		
Is there a prepayment penalty?		
If so, how much is it?		
How long does the penalty period last?		
Are extra principal payments allowed?		
Is the lock-in agreement in writing?		
Is there a fee to lock-in?		
When does the lock-in occur - at application, approval or another time?		
How long will the lock-in last?		

When the rate drops before closing, can you lock-in at a lower rate?		
If adjustable rate - What is the maximum the rate could be next year?		
What are the rate and payment caps each year and over the life of the loan?		
What is the frequency of rate change and any changes to the monthly payment?		

6. Compare

Once you have gotten all of the pertinent information (preferably in writing) for the same loan amount, compare loan terms and costs. Be sure to compare quotes for a fixed rate mortgage to each other and quotes for an adjustable rate mortgage to each other.

7. Decide whether to pay points or a higher interest rate.

One point is equal to 1% of the mortgage amount. For each point you pay you are lowering the interest rate. A lower interest rate, of course, means a lower monthly payment. Experts say if you plan to stay in the house 5-7 years it usually makes sense to pay the points because the lower interest rate will save you money in the long run. If you plan to be in the house less than 5 years experts say it is usually more cost-effective to take the higher interest rate.

8. Negotiate the best deal.

Ask if the lender or broker will waive or reduce one or more of its fees or agree to a lower rate or fewer points. You will want to make sure that the lender or broker is not agreeing to lower one fee while raising another or agreeing to lower the rate while raising points.

There is no harm in asking lenders or brokers if they can give better terms than the original ones they quoted or than those you have found elsewhere.

Note: On any given day, lenders and brokers may offer different prices for the same loan terms to different consumers, even if those consumers have the same loan qualifications. The most likely reason for this difference in price is that loan officers and brokers are often allowed to keep some or all of this difference as extra compensation.

Generally, the difference between the lowest available price for a loan product and any higher price that the borrower agrees to pay is an overage. When overages occur, they are built into the prices quoted to consumers. They can occur in both fixed and variable-rate loans and can be in the form of points, fees, or the interest rate. Whether quoted to you by a loan officer or a broker, the price of any loan may contain overages.

9. Lock in the interest rate.

Once you are satisfied with the terms you have negotiated, you may want to obtain a written lock-in from the lender or broker. The lock-in should include the rate that you have agreed upon, the period the lock-in lasts, and the number of points to be paid. The lender may charge a fee for locking in the loan rate. This fee may be refundable at closing. Lock-ins can protect you from rate increases while your loan is being processed; if rates fall, however, you could end up with a less favorable rate. Should that happen, try to negotiate a compromise with the lender or broker.

20

Get the best refinancing deal

Experts say you should consider refinancing your mortgage if you can get a rate that is at least one percentage point lower than your existing mortgage rate.

1. Determine your credit score.

Since your credit score has a big impact on the interest rate you pay, it is a good idea to have as high a credit score as possible. See Chapter 17 for a full discussion on the definition of credit scoring, how a credit score is determined, how to get a copy of your credit report and how to improve your credit score.

2. Review commonly used mortgage terms.

See Chapter 19 – 9 Ways to save when seeking a mortgage.

3. Consider how long you plan to remain in your home.

Let us look at an example. Let's say that by refinancing your mortgage you save $250 per month in mortgage payments. The cost of refinancing is $5000. Therefore, it would take you 20 months ($5000÷ $250 = 20 months) in order to break even on the mortgage refinance.

Therefore, if you remain in your home for at least 20 months you will have recovered your costs for refinancing. Of course, after 20 months you really begin to realize significant savings.

4. Shop for best interest rates and terms.

Visit a few online lenders and get some figures based on your personal situation. Many lenders and brokers only require you to fill out a brief informational sheet in order to provide you with a loan quote. Most do not require a credit check at this stage, so there is no harm in getting more than a few quotes. A company such as **www.lowermybills.com** will give quotes from up to 4 lenders.

5. Consider using your original lender.

They may give you a discount on some of the fees in order to keep your business, particularly if you have made your payments on time, and if the work relating to the mortgage closing is still current.

6. Use your original appraiser.

Since they have all of your specifications on your house, they may be willing to give you a discount on the appraisal fee.

7. Use your original title company.

Ask them for a "reissue rate" which is lower than the standard rate. Since they have all of the paperwork from the original title work, they will usually grant your request.

8. Consider 15-year rather than 30- year mortgage.

At 7.50% on a $100,000 loan you would save $84,854 if you got a 15-year mortgage instead of a 30-year mortgage.

To calculate your savings on a 15-year mortgage compared to a 30-year mortgage go to **www.bankrate.com**. Click on "Calculations".

9. Decide whether to pay points or a higher interest rate.

One point is equal to 1% of the mortgage amount. For each point you pay you are lowering the interest rate. A lower interest rate, of course, means a lower monthly payment. Experts say if you plan to stay in the house 5-7 years, it usually makes sense to pay the points because the lower interest rate will save you money in the long run. If you plan to be in the house less than 5 years experts say it is usually more cost-effective to take the higher interest rate.

21

Pocket an extra $40 per month

If you have taken a mortgage and you made less than a 20 percent down payment, your lender may have required you to have Private Mortgage Insurance (PMI). PMI protects the lender if you default on the loan. While this is a good way to get into your first house with a small down payment, the amount you pay for PMI does nothing to reduce the principle amount of the loan.

There is good news -

You can have your PMI canceled when you reach 20 percent equity in your home based on the original property value.

1. Check your annual escrow account statement to find out exactly how much you are paying each year for PMI.

On a $100,000 loan with 10 percent down ($10,000), PMI might cost you **$40 a month**. If you can cancel the PMI, you can save **$480** a year and many thousands of dollars over the life of the loan.

2. Contact your lender or mortgage servicing company to find out when your PMI can be canceled.

3. Get your house appraised.

Since home prices have gone up substantially, you may have reached the 20 percent equity more quickly that originally projected.

4. Ask your lender to drop the PMI.

5. Determine what you are going to do with the extra $40 per month.

22

Get the best deal on a home equity loan

With home values having appreciated significantly over the past few years, you may want to take some of the equity out to pay for college, do some home improvement, pay off some bills, etc. One way to do that is to get a home equity loan. Here are some tips for getting the best deal:

1. Determine your credit score.

Since your credit score has a big impact on the interest rate you will pay, it is a good idea to have as high a credit score as possible. See Chapter 17 for a full discussion on the definition of credit scoring, how a credit score is determined, how to get a copy of your credit report and how to improve your credit score.

2. Get information on various loan programs.

Contact several lenders, not just the ones that send you mail, call you, or knock on your door. Talk with banks, savings and loans, credit unions, mortgage companies, and mortgage brokers. (Note: brokers don't lend money, they help arrange loans.)

Information to collect:

o   Annual Percentage Rate (APR).

o   Application or loan processing fee.

o   Origination or underwriting fee.

o   Lender or funding fee.

o   Appraisal fee.

o   Document preparation.

o   Recording fees.

o   Broker fees (which may be quoted as points).

3. Compare.

Compare all of the information you have collected about various loan programs.

4. Negotiate with more than one lender.

Don't be afraid to make lenders and brokers compete for your business by letting them know that you are shopping for the best deal. Ask each lender to lower the points, fees or the interest rate. And ask each to meet – or beat – the terms of the other lenders.

5. Read the loan closing papers carefully.

If the loan isn't what you expected or wanted, don't sign the loan. Either negotiate changes or walk away. You also generally have the right to cancel the deal for any reason – and without penalty – within three days after signing the loan papers. The lender must return any money you have paid up to that point.

23

Slash your property taxes

Your house is your castle, or at least it seems that way when you receive your tax bill.

—Creative Wit

Based on research done by the National Taxpayer's Union, between 30 and 60% of all U.S property is assessed at a higher value than it is worth. Additionally, approximately 50% of those who contest their tax bill have their assessment reduced. Order the booklet "How to Fight Property Taxes" from the National Taxpayer's Union at **www.ntu.org**. The booklet costs $6.95. Happy contesting!

24

Save thousands when buying a new car

"Wait! Come back! I think I can lower the price another thousand."

Picture a car salesman yelling this to you as you are leaving the dealer showroom. This scene is not too far-fetched. By following these steps you will be sure to save lots of money the next time you buy a new car.

1. Verify your credit score.

Since your credit score has a big impact on the interest rate you will pay, it is a good idea to have as high a credit score as possible. See Chapter 17 for a full discussion on the definition of credit scoring, how a credit score is determined, how to get a copy of your credit report and how to improve your credit score.

2. Determine how much you can afford to pay each month.

3. Research the dealer's price for the car and options.

It's easier to get the best price when you know what the dealer paid for the vehicle. You can find a list of standard and optional features and their wholesale costs for each model at **www. consumerreports.org**.

4. Find out if the manufacturer is offering rebates.

This can dramatically reduce the price of the vehicle. You can learn about rebates at **www.carsdirect.com**.

5. Consider the fuel use.

www.fueleconomy.gov has gas mileage estimates for 1985 - current model year cars.

6. Consider the insurance costs.

Check with you insurance company to find out what the premium will be. If the car is a likely target for thieves, for example, it could raise the insurance costs and influence your decision on the type of car to purchase.

7. Arrange your own financing.

This is one of the three ways the dealer makes money (the other two are in selling you the vehicle and on the trade-in). You can save money and improve your negotiating position if you already have your financing in hand when you walk into the dealership. Check the interest rates at your credit union, your bank, or other organization with which you are affiliated. You can also check rates on the Internet at **www.lowermybills.com**

8. Time your visit.

Go during the week, when there is not much activity, preferably when it is raining.

9. Negotiate your trade-in separately.

This is one of the three ways the dealer makes money (the other two are in selling you the vehicle and providing the financing). You can save money and improve your negotiating position if you negotiate your trade-in as a separate transaction. Get the price quote for the new car in writing before you discuss the trade-in. This way the dealer does not discount the new car and then subtract that same amount from what he allows you for the trade-in.

10. Avoid expensive "Extras".

Avoid high-profit, low–value extras such as credit insurance, extended service contracts, auto club memberships, rust proofing and upholstery finishes.

25

Buy a previously owned car
(Without getting taken for a ride)

There is a sucker born every minute.

—P.T. Barnum, Carnival King

Because new vehicles lose so much of their value as soon as they are purchased, previously owned cars are a smart financial alternative. Today, thanks to manufacturing and maintenance advances, used vehicles are better than ever. There are a number of ways you can avoid being a sucker when it comes to buying a previously owned car.

1. Verify your credit score.

Since your credit score has a big impact on the interest rate you will pay, it is a good idea to have as high a credit score as possible. See Chapter 17 for a full discussion on the definition of credit scoring, how a credit score is determined, how to get a copy of your credit report and how to improve your credit score.

2. Determine how much you can afford to pay each month.

3. Research what the dealer paid for the car.

It's easier to get the best price when you know what the dealer paid for the vehicle. Check the National Automobile Dealers Association (NADA) Guide to get prices. You can get a copy at the library or online at **www.nada.com**.

When you check NADA you will see three sets of prices:

Wholesale	Loan	Retail
$8459	$8000	$9800

Wholesale price – This is the price you can expect to receive from a dealer at trade-in. This is the maximum price that the dealer paid for the car. (He probably paid less.)

Loan price - This is the amount a bank will be willing to loan on that vehicle. This is usually the retail amount of the vehicle minus 20% that is your down payment.

Retail price – This is the "asking price" that the dealer has assigned to the car.

Use the back of the NADA book to add or deduct for options in the car, its condition and its mileage. These items will increase or decrease the price.

Key Point: When it comes to negotiating the price, your objective is to get as close to the wholesale price as possible.

4. Arrange your own financing.

This is one of the three ways the dealer makes money (the other two are in selling you the vehicle and on the trade-in). You can save money and improve your negotiating position if you already have your financing in hand when you walk into the dealership.

Check the interest rates at your credit union, your bank, or other organization with which you are affiliated. You can also check rates on the Internet at **www.bankrate.com**.

5. Time your visit to the dealership.

Go during the week, when there is not much activity. Since the salespeople are not busy, you will be in a much better negotiating position.

6. Get a Carfax Vehicle Report.

CARFAX Vehicle History Reports reveal the truth about used cars and they provide important background information to unearth hidden problems in a vehicle's past that may affect its safety and resale value. The reports reveal:

- o If the vehicle has been totaled in an accident/salvaged.
- o If there has been flood damage.
- o If the odometer has been rolled back.
- o Lemon histories.
- o Junked titles.
- o State emissions inspection results.
- o Lien activity.
- o How the vehicle has been used (taxi, rental, lease, etc.).

To get a copy of a report on a specific vehicle go to **www.carfax. com**.

7. Consider fuel use.

www.fueleconomy.gov has gas mileage estimates for 1985 - to current model year cars.

8. Consider insurance costs.

Check with your insurance company to find out what the premium will be. If the car is a likely target for thieves, for example, it could raise the insurance costs and influence your decision on the type of car to purchase.

9. Thoroughly inspect the car.

Take a look. Make sure the body parts line up, the paint matches, doors open and close easily, and that tires are wearing evenly.

Lift the hood. Check under the hood for leaky hoses, worn belts, and dirty oil. Automatic transmission fluid should be clear and reddish, and not smell burned. Radiator water should have a light yellow or green color.

Take a seat. Turn the ignition key to accessory and make sure all of the warning lights and gauges work. Start the car and check all lights and accessories and make sure no warning lights remain lit on the dashboard. Pay close attention to the airbag indicator lights. If these lights fail to illuminate as you start the car, or stay lit after the car is running, it is a warning that the car's airbags are not functioning correctly.

Perform a safety check. Try on the seat belt and take a test drive to ensure that you are comfortable while driving the vehicle. Make sure head restraints, roof structures, and windshield designs do not interfere with your ability to see clearly. Test the vehicle at dusk or early evening to determine your comfort with the visibility provided by the headlamps. If you already have a child safety seat, install it to check for compatibility.

Hit the road. Take the vehicle up to 35-40 MPH. Make sure shifting is smooth and steering is straight. When braking, a pull to the left or the right could indicate a brake problem. The steering wheel should not shimmy at high speeds and cornering should be smooth.

Consumer Reports.org has joined with CarFax to develop A Guide to Inspecting Used Cars. To get your free copy go to **www.carfax.com** and click on "Inspection Guide".

10. Keep the car overnight.

This gives you additional time to check the car out, and even have your mechanic put the car up on the lift and check it out.

11. Avoid expensive "Extras".

Avoid high-profit, low–value extras such as credit insurance and extended service contracts.

26

Save $250 per year on your auto insurance

Here's why insurance companies
Are mostly indestructible:
The cost of damages most times
Is less than the deductible.

—G. Sterling Leiby

If you own a car there is a high probability that you are paying too much for your insurance. There is an even higher probability that by taking a few simple steps you can save up to 30% in premiums.

1. Understand commonly used auto insurance terms:

Anti-Theft Device — Devices designed either to reduce the chance an auto will be vandalized or stolen, or assist in its recovery. Examples include car alarms, keyless entry, starter disablers, motion detectors, parts of the vehicle etched with the Vehicle Identification Number, and recovery systems.

Assigned Risk — A risk not ordinarily acceptable to insurers which is, according to state law, assigned to insurers participating in a plan in which the insurers agree to accept their share of these risks.

Basic Limits of Liability — The least amount of liability coverage that can be purchased, which is generally equivalent to the minimum amount required by state law. In determining rates, a carrier will use the basic limits to develop the base rates. If an insured person wants higher limits, the carrier applies an increased limits factor to the base rate in calculating the new premium for the increased coverage.

Bodily Injury Liability — Legal liability for causing physical injury or death to another.

Collision Insurance — This covers loss to the insured person's own auto caused by its collision with another vehicle or object.

Combined Single Limit — Bodily Injury and Property Damage coverage expressed as one single amount of coverage.

Comprehensive Coverage — Covers damage to a vehicle caused by an event other than a collision or overturn. Examples include fire, theft, vandalism, and falling objects.

Continuous Coverage or Continuous Liability Insurance — Continuous coverage refers to the length of time you have maintained insurance on your vehicle.

Covered Person — This refers to the individuals (named insured, spouse, resident relatives, etc.) insured under a policy contract.

Customized Equipment/Special Equipment — Items not included in standard insurance options available for cars. These may include extra electronic equipment, special paint or exterior items, or amenities added to the inside of a van or truck.

Deductible — The amount an insured person must pay before the insurance company pays the remainder of each covered loss, up to the policy limits.

Defensive Driver Course — These are classes either offered through or approved by Departments of Motor Vehicles to enhance driving skills. These courses may make drivers eligible for discounts on their premiums. Courses taken for traffic school because of a moving violation are not eligible.

Drive-Other-Car Endorsement — Optional coverage that broadens the definition of a covered auto to include non-owned vehicles the insured person operates.

Driver Education — State accredited educational course that consists of at least 30 hours of professional classroom instruction.

Driver Training — State accredited training course that consists of at least six hours of behind-the-wheel professional instruction.

Effective Date/Inception Date — The date that coverage begins on an insurance policy.

Expiration Date — The date your coverage ends. There is usually a time of day associated with this date, for example, an expiration date of 5/1/2002 at 12:01a.m. This means your coverage ends one minute after midnight on the date listed.

Extended Non-Owner Liability — An endorsement that provides broader liability coverage for specifically named people operating any non-owned automobile or trailer. It covers non-owned autos, use of autos to carry people or property for a fee, and individuals driving employer-furnished cars who do not own vehicles themselves.

Family Automobile Policy — Now replaced by the Personal Auto Policy, the Family Auto Policy was a package policy in which both liability and physical damage protection to an insured's vehicle was offered under one policy.

Financial Ratings — Financial ratings reflect a rating organization's opinion on the financial strength and ability to meet ongoing obligations to policyholders. The ratings organizations most commonly identified with the insurance industry are AM Best, Standard & Poor's and Moody's.

First Party Benefits — This pays policyholders and others covered by the policy in the event of injury, no matter who caused the accident. The benefits can include medical expenses, loss of income, funeral and death benefits. This may also be called Personal Injury Protection.

Gap Insurance — If you are making lease or loan payments and you experience a total loss, there may be a difference (gap) between the market value of your vehicle and what you still owe on it. This optional coverage pays the difference.

Good Student Discount — A premium discount for students with high scholastic grades. Some statistical research has shown a relationship between good grades and safe driving.

Lapse in Coverage/Policy Lapse — A point in time when a policy has been canceled or terminated for failure to pay the premium, or when the policy contract is void for other reasons.

Medical Payments — This pays for medical and funeral expenses incurred in an auto accident, regardless of fault. It will also cover injuries sustained by passengers in your car, or while you are operating someone else's car (with their permission), in addition to injuries you or your family members incur when you're pedestrians.

Multi-car discount — A discount offered by some insurance companies for those with more than one vehicle insured on the same policy. In some cases, if you drive a company car insured by your company, your own insurance company may give you the multi-car discount.

Motor Vehicle Record (MVR) — A motor vehicle record, also referred to as DL printout, or MVR, contains information obtained from an individual's driver license application, abstracts of convictions and accidents.

Named Insured — Any person, firm or corporation designated by name as the insured person(s) in a policy. Others may be protected by policy definition even though their names aren't on the policy, such as other drivers operating (with consent) the named insured's covered auto.

Named Non-Owner Policy — A policy endorsement for one who operates any non-owned automobile on a regular basis, such as driving a car provided by one's employer.

No-Fault Insurance — Many states have enacted auto accident compensation laws permitting auto accident victims to collect directly from their own insurance companies for medical and hospital expenses regardless of who was at fault in the accident. Although there are many legal variations of no-fault insurance, most states still allow people to sue the negligent party if the amount of damages exceeds a certain state-determined threshold. (See "Threshold Level.")

Non-Owned Auto — Any vehicle that is not owned, borrowed, or leased by the insured, and which is used primarily for a business purpose.

Per Occurrence Limit — This refers to the cap amount an insurance company will pay for all claims arising from a single incident. In an automobile accident, it comprises bodily injuries sustained by all parties. When Bodily Injury coverage is purchased in split limits, the second limit is the "per occurrence" limit: e.g. $100,000(per person)/$300,000(per occurrence)

Per Person Limit — This refers to the cap amount an insurance company will pay for any one person's injuries arising from a single incident. In an automobile accident, it comprises bodily injuries sustained by each person. When Bodily Injury is purchased in split limits, the first limit is the "per person" limit: e.g. $100,000(per person)/$300,000(per occurrence)

Personal Auto Policy — The most common auto insurance policy sold today. Often referred to as "PAP," this policy is written in simple wording and provides coverage for liability, medical payments, uninsured/underinsured motorist coverage, and physical damage protection.

Personal Injury Protection — The name usually given to no-fault benefits in states that have enacted mandatory or optional no-fault auto insurance laws. Personal Injury Protection (PIP) usually includes benefits for medical expenses, loss of income from work, essential services, accidental death, funeral expenses, and survivor benefits.

Physical Damage — Damage to your covered vehicle from perils including (but not limited to) collision or upset with another vehicle object, fire, vandalism and theft.

Policy — The written documents of a contract for insurance between the insurance company and the insured. Such documents include forms, endorsements, riders and attachments.

Policy Period — The period of time in which a policy is in effect. (For example, six months or one year).

Policyholder — One who maintains ownership in an insurance policy. This may refer to the policy owner or those covered under the policy. See also Named Insured.

Preferred Risk — Any risk considered to be better than the standard risk on which the premium rate was calculated.

Premium — The price of insurance an insured person pays for a specified risk for a specified period of time.

Private Passenger Automobile — A four-wheeled motor vehicle that is subject to motor vehicle registration and used for private personal use.

Pro Rata Cancellation — Termination of an insurance contract before the policy expiration date on which the premium returned to the insured person is adjusted in proportion to the amount of time the policy was in effect.

Property Damage Liability Insurance — Protection against liability for damage to another's tangible property, including loss of use. Although this coverage is different than liability for bodily injury to another person, Bodily Injury and Property Damage Liability protection are generally written together.

Renewal — The process of keeping an active policy in force through the issuance of a renewal policy.

Rental Reimbursement — This optional coverage will reimburse you for a rental car if your vehicle is disabled due to a covered loss. This coverage will pay all or part of your rental car costs.

Safe Driver Plan — A rating system that assigns points for traffic convictions and certain accidents. Similar to a merit-rating plan, each point increases the surcharge percentage to the baseline rates.

Split Limit — Any insurance coverage with separately stated limits for different types of coverage. Example: an automobile liability policy of 100/300/50 provides a maximum of $100,000 bodily injury coverage per person, $300,000 bodily injury coverage per accident, and a property damage limit of $50,000 per accident.

Stacking of Limits — The application of more than one policy limit to the same loss or occurrence. In some jurisdictions, courts have required stacking of limits when multiple policies, or multiple policy periods, cover an occurrence. For example, Uninsured motorist bodily injury limits of $100,000/300,000 on two policies owned by the same person may be added together to pay a loss. In this event, the total amount of coverage available for an accident would be $200,000/600,000.

Term — The length of time for which a policy or bond is in force.

Threshold Level — Under some no-fault insurance laws, the threshold level represents the degree of injury a claimant must establish before being allowed to sue the negligent party. The threshold may be verbal (regarding the severity of the injuries) or a dollar amount ($10,000), or both. For example, with a threshold of $5,000, an injured person may sue if his/her injuries and other economic damages (rehabilitation expenses, loss of income, etc.) exceed $5,000.

Towing and Labor Costs — This endorsement, which is added to the physical damage coverage, provides reimbursement up to a specified limit to tow your vehicle or pay for on-site labor costs.

Transportation Expenses — Subject to a daily and maximum dollar limit, this coverage (under the physical damage portion of an automobile policy) pays for transportation expenses incurred by the named insured only in the event of theft of an entire covered auto. Coverage generally begins after a stated minimum waiting period.

Uninsured Motorists Bodily Injury — Uninsured motorist's bodily injury coverage (which must be offered in most states) pays for a covered person's bodily injuries of which an uninsured or hit-and-run motorist is legally liable, but unable to pay.

Underinsured Motorists Bodily Injury — Underinsured motorists bodily injury coverage (which must be offered in most states) pays for a covered person's bodily injuries of which a person with not enough insurance is legally liable.

Uninsured Motorists Property Damage — Uninsured Motorist Property Damage Liability coverage pays for property damages caused by uninsured drivers.

Unearned Premium — The portion of your premium remaining on your policy term. For example, with a six-month premium, at the end of the first month of the premium period, five-sixths of the premium is unearned by the insurance company.

Usage — This refers to the primary function or purpose in which you intend to operate your vehicle. For example, if you primarily drive your car to and from work, the usage is considered "commute; "if you're self-employed and you primarily drive to see customers, the usage is considered "business;" if you're retired, your usage is considered "pleasure."

Waiver of Collision Deductible — This option pays your collision deductible when you carry collision coverage on a vehicle that is damaged by an uninsured or hit-and-run motorist who is at fault. Coverage applies only when there is actual physical contact and when you can identify the uninsured driver or vehicle.

Whole Dollar Premium — Generally, insurance premiums are rounded to the nearest dollar; an amount of 51 cents or more being rounded up to the next dollar, and any amount less than that being dropped.

2. Raise your deductible.

Deductibles represent the amount of money you pay before you make a claim. By requesting higher deductibles on collision and comprehensive (fire and theft) coverage, you can lower your costs substantially. For example, increasing your deductible from $200 to $500 could reduce your collision cost by as much as 30%. Since the national average annual premium is $687 this can save you $206 per year.

3. Insure your teenager on your policy.

This way he/she gets your discounts.

4. Ask for a Good Student Discount.

If your teenager has at least a "B" average many insurance companies will give a Good Student Discount.

5. Comparison shop.

Since prices for the same coverage can vary by hundreds of dollars, it pays to shop around. Ask your friends, check the yellow pages or call your state insurance department. You can also check consumer guides, insurance agents or companies.

This will give you an idea of price ranges and tell you which companies or agents have the lowest prices. But don't shop price alone. The insurer you select should offer both fair prices and excellent service. Quality personal service may cost a bit more, but provides added conveniences. So talk to a number of insurers to get a feeling for the quality of their service. Ask them what they would do to lower your costs. Check the financial ratings of the companies too. Then, when you have narrowed the field to three insurers, get price quotes.

6. Drop coverage on older cars.

If your car is 5 or more years old, you may be paying more in premiums than the insurance company would pay if you had a claim. If that is the case, you may be well advised to drop the collision coverage and bank the savings.

7. Avoid duplicate medical coverage.

If you have adequate health insurance, you may be paying for duplicate medical coverage in your auto policy. In some states, eliminating this coverage could lower your personal injury protection (PIP) cost by up to 40%.

8. Drive a "Low-Profile" car.

Before you buy a new or used car, check into insurance costs. Cars that are expensive to repair, or are favorite targets for thieves have much higher insurance costs. Go to **www.hwysafety.org** and click on "Injury, Collision and Theft Loss" to see how your car is ranked.

9. Drive less.

Some companies offer discounts to motorists who drive less than a predetermined number of miles a year. Consider using public transportation, a carpool or vanpool to commute to work.

10. Seek a multi-policy discount.

Some companies give a discount if you have more than one policy with them.

11. Seek a discount for seat belts and air bags.

12. Take a defensive driving course.

13. Ask for a discount based on your profession.

Some professions (such as engineers) qualify for discounted premiums because they have been found to have fewer claims. Ask your insurance company if your profession qualifies for a discount.

14. Ask for a discount based on your credit score.

Some companies use the credit score to establish premiums. If you have a high credit score, ask for a discount.

15. Ask for other discounts.

Examples are:

- o Safe driver – no claims accidents in three years, no moving violations in three years.

- o Over 50 years of age.

- o Anti-theft devices and Anti-lock brakes.

27

Cut bank fees in half

Beware of little expenses; a small leak will sink a great ship.

—Benjamin Franklin

1. Order checks and deposit slips online rather than through the bank.

Order at **www.123checksonline.com** and **www.checksunlimited.com**.

2. Use a bank that offers free checking.

It may be possible to achieve this at your current bank by placing all of your accounts there or by linking all of your accounts. Call your bank and ask.

3. Join a credit union.

Unlike a bank that has to show a profit for its shareholders, a credit union returns any profits to its members in the form of lower interest rates, lower fees and better services. To find a credit union for which you are eligible for membership and that is right for you go to **www.ncua.gov** and click on "Credit Union Data".

4. Connect your money market account to your checking account.

There is no charge for this, and since banks typically clear the largest checks first, this can save you the bounced-check charge of at least $25 — $30 if you accidentally overdraw your checking account.

5. Never use a foreign ATM.

If you make a withdrawal from a bank other than your own, your bank will charge you $1.50 and the bank from which you made the withdrawal will charge you $1.50. That means that on a $20.00 withdrawal, you will pay a 15% surcharge for the privilege of getting your own money.

6. Balance your checkbook and reconcile your stat statement each month.

This will enable you to spot errors and avoid potential overdrafts.

28

Reduce life insurance cost by 30%

Somebody once said "Life insurance is what keeps a man poor all of his life so he can die rich."

You can have the proper amount of insurance without being poor.

1. Understand commonly used life insurance terms:

Accelerated Benefits Rider — Allows for payment of some portion of the face amount of the insurance policy if the policyholder develops a terminal illness or injury.

Accidental Death and Dismemberment — Provides for payment of an additional benefit over and above the face amount of the policy when death occurs by accident.

Annual Renewal Term — Provides coverage for one year and allows the policy owner to renew his or her coverage each year, without having to prove he/she is insurable.

Beneficiary — Person to whom proceeds of a policy will go when the policyholder dies.

Contingent beneficiary — Person or persons to receive proceeds from a policy in the event the original beneficiary is not alive.

Conversion Privilege — Allows the policy-owner, before an original policy expires, to elect to have a new policy issued that will allow the insurance to continue. For example, let's say you take out a term policy that runs to age 65, and you could have a conversion privilege that allows you to convert to whole-life insurance at that point.

Decreasing Term insurance — The face amount decreases while the premium remains level.

Disability Income Rider — Provides periodic income should the insured become disabled due to illness or injury.

Face Amount — The amount the insurance company will pay to a beneficiary if the policyholder dies.

Insurance Company Ratings — There are five major insurance industry rating services: A.M. Best, Standard and Poor's, Moody's, Fitch and Weiss. They provide information on a company's financial performance, stability, their ability to pay claims and more. Check out a company's rating before doing business with them. Obviously, the higher the rating the more stable the company.

Increasing Term Insurance — The death benefit increases periodically over the policy's term. This is usually purchased as a cost of living rider to a whole life policy.

Level Term Insurance — The face value and premiums remain unchanged from the date the policy is issued to the date the policy expires.

Other Insured Rider — Covers an eligible family member other than the insured and is attached to the base policy.

Mortality Table — Projections of how many people at what age will die during a given year. Insurance companies use these projections to establish premiums.

Preferred Risk — A person whose physical condition, occupation and mode of living and other characteristics indicate that he/she will live longer than someone of a lesser physical condition, or a riskier occupation.

Premium — Payment to keep a policy in force.

Primary Beneficiary — The person who will get the proceeds first if the insured dies.

Proceeds — Net amount the company pays if the insured dies.

Rider — Adds something to the policy.

Secondary Beneficiary — An alternate beneficiary designated to receive proceeds in the event the original beneficiary dies first.

Smoker Ratings — Insurers charge a lower premium to buyers who do not smoke. If you smoked previously but quit, most companies will charge a non-smoker premium if you have not smoked for a year. Be truthful. Blood tests that are used detect nicotine use.

Standard Risk — Person who can get insurance without paying an extra premium.

Sub-Standard Risk — An under-average risk because of physical condition, family or personal history of disease, occupation, residence in unhealthy climate or dangerous habits.

Suicide Clause — Most policies provide that if the insured commits suicide within a specified period, generally two years, after the issue date the company will not pay the face amount of the policy. Instead, the company will return premiums paid to the estate of the deceased.

Term Insurance — Protection during a limited number of years and expiring at the end of that time.

Term of policy — Period that the policy runs.

Uninsurable Risk — One not acceptable for insurance dues to excessive risk.

Waiver of Premium — Provision that exempts the policyholder from paying premiums after he/she has been disabled for a period of time, usually six months.

2. Don't buy life insurance if you don't need it.

The purpose of life insurance is to replace the breadwinner's income if he/she dies before being able to build up sufficient financial assets. So, if you have someone depending on you to earn a certain amount of income during a period of time life insurance is the way to go. Let's say you are a young husband at age 30 and your wife is a stay-at-home mom. You have little or no savings, small children, a mortgage, and some bills as a result of buying furniture and appliances to establish a household. If you were to die your family would be financially devastated. You are a prime candidate for life insurance. So you take out a 30-year term insurance policy for the appropriate amount. Let us fast forward for a moment. You are now 60 years old. The children have grown up and have finished school, the mortgage is paid off and other bills have been paid off. For the past 30 years you have been investing a portion of your earnings and you have accumulated a sizeable nest egg. At this point, there is no further need for life insurance. The insurance policy that you took out 30 years ago has enabled you to buy time by protecting your family while you were accumulating the nest egg.

On the other hand, if you are single with no dependents or retired and living on investments or retirement income you probably do not need life insurance.

3. Determine how much you need.

If you decide that you do need insurance, the next step is to figure out how much you need. Go to **www.bankrate.com/ brm/insurance_home.asp** and click on "Insurance". You will answer a series of questions and at the end you will receive a recommendation on the right amount of insurance for you.

4. Check your credit score.

If there are problems clear them up before applying. If not, you could wind up either being denied coverage or charged a higher premium. The higher premium represents the company's concern that you may not pay the premium and let the policy drop. If that happens the company stands to lose money because they will have paid the agent a commission as high as 90% - 100% of the first year's premium. Read Chapter 17 – 8 ways to improve your credit score.

5. Shop around.

There are over 1500 companies that sell life insurance and premiums vary by hundred of dollars for the same amount of coverage. For example, for $100,000 worth of term life insurance for a 35- year- old male I recently found annual premiums that ranged from $886 to $2194. Some places to shop:

o   Companies that do not pay their sales people a commission. Some examples are: USAA Life Insurance Company 1-800-531-8000, Ameritas Life Insurance Company 1-800-745-1112, Southland Life Insurance Company 1-800-872-7542 and American Life of New York 1-212-399-5555

o   The Internet at **www.insure.com**. They will search from a database of over 90 companies and give you instant quotes from the lowest priced companies. You can also call them at 1-800-556-9393 and seek unbiased advice from a salaried counselor. Afterwards, you are free to buy from the company of your choice.

Words of caution as you shop:

With the advancements in medical technology and healthier lifestyles, people are living longer. For example, twenty years ago a 40-year old man was expected to live to be 73. Today a man who is 40 years old is expected to live to be 78. This means that instead of using the 1980 mortality tables companies are now starting to use 2000 mortality tables. This also means they are starting to reduce the premiums they charge. In fact, experts predict that the premiums on term insurance will drop as much as 30 percent in the next few years. Some companies, however, may still be using the 1980 mortality tables with the shorter life expectancy and thus still charging the higher premiums. This is perfectly legal since they have until 2009 to fully implement the use of the new mortality tables. In the meantime, when you get a premium quote, make sure the company is using the 2000 tables.

6. Buy term insurance.

There are two kinds of policies: Term and whole life (or permanent or cash value). Term is pure insurance for a set number of years, 10, 15, 20, or 30 and it only pays a death benefit. Whole life, on the other hand, may provide interest and dividends. Since there are no dividends or interest involved, term insurance is generally less expensive than whole life.

So the husband in Tip # 1 would be better served to buy the appropriate amount of term insurance to protect his family during their most vulnerable period and to invest the extra money into something like a stock mutual fund that will enable him to be financially secure later in life.

7. Keep insurance separate from investments.

One reason for some of the consumer's confusion about life insurance is that some companies combine investments with life insurance. In order to do a proper comparison, it makes sense to keep the two separate because they are designed to meet two distinct needs.

When we purchase most items we consider the cost per unit. For example, when we purchase ground beef we look at the cost per pound, when we purchase gasoline we look at the price per gallon. When we are considering term life insurance we likewise should look at the cost per unit. The way to evaluate term life insurance is to determine the cost per $1000 of coverage.

In order to do that you divide the annual premium you are quoted by the amount of coverage you have determined that you need. For example, if you decide that you need $700,000 in coverage and the premium you are quoted is $3700, the cost per $1000 of coverage would be $5.28 ($3700 ÷ $700).

Using this method you are now ready to compare prices without getting into the "mumbo jumbo" about projected rate of return on your investment and building cash value and other terms that tend to distort what you are really trying to do - protect your family in case you die before you accumulate adequate assets.

8. Get group insurance through your employer.

Some employers offer free life insurance as an employee benefit. Other times the employer may offer a designated amount free and the employee has the option of purchasing additional coverage. Since this is group coverage the premiums are usually real low and it's a good deal for the employee. In addition to the group policy at work you may want to consider buying an individual policy. If you have all of your insurance through your employer and lose your job, you have no coverage. Some companies will allow you to convert to an individual policy should your employment be terminated, but I can tell you the premiums would give you a shock.

9. If you have a specific medical conditions seek a company that specializes.

For example, some companies specialize in insuring people with diabetes, while others are more lenient when it comes to the relationship between height and weight. Seek out the best companies for your situation. The best way to save money and time is to have an Internet company such as **www.insure.com** do the search for you.

10. Quit smoking.

In addition to saving $1800.00 per year (a pack per day @ $5/ pack x 365 days), you will also save on life insurance premiums. Most companies charge twice as much to insure a smoker as they do a nonsmoker.

11. Skip the insurance on children.

Remember: the purpose of life insurance is to replace lost income. As much as you love your children, you probably are not dependent on them economically.

12. Ask for a change in rating class.

Let's say you took out a policy four years ago right after you learned that you had high blood pressure. The company did a physical examination and because of your high blood pressure they placed you in a certain rating class with a higher premium than you would have been charged had you not had high blood pressure. Let's further say that during the last four years you have taken control of your health, lost weight, exercised, taken your medication and now your blood pressure is normal. Under those circumstances you can go back and ask them to review your medical status and put you in a rating class with a lower premium.

13. Make fewer premium payments.

The fewer payments you make in a year, the lower your annual premium. Some companies add as much as 20% to the annual premium if you make monthly payments. You can reduce the total amount you pay by paying quarterly, semiannually or annually.

14. Just say "No" to mortgage insurance.

Many times when you purchase a house, insurance companies will approach you to sell you mortgage insurance. If you have correctly determined the amount of insurance (if any) that you need and bought term insurance, your family is already adequately covered and you do not need to buy a separate policy to cover your mortgage.

29

16 ways to cut prescription drug costs

At today's prices for medication, **any** pill is a bitter pill to swallow.

—Creative Wit

As anyone who takes a prescription drug knows, the prices have skyrocketed. According to the Employee Benefit Research Institute, prescription drug expenditures have grown at double-digit rates during almost every year since 1980, accelerating to 14.1% in 1997. Even if your health insurance pays for medications, you may have hefty co-payments or deductibles. Nonetheless, there are ways to stretch your prescription-drug dollar. Let us discuss some of them.

1. Know what your medical insurance or managed health care plan covers.

Before you sign up for a plan, check what your co-payments for prescription drugs will be as well as the maximum amount the plan will pay in a year. Also find out if your health plan has a formulary - that is, a list of drugs that they will cover. A health plan with a closed formulary pays only for certain pre-approved drugs. If the drug you need is not on the list, you pay the whole cost. Open formularies offer most drugs, but the prices vary. If your plan has a closed formulary, you may be able to request an exception by having your doctor fill out a form. But you may have to go through an appeals process.

2. Get free samples.

Drug sales representatives are always leaving samples in doctors' offices for the doctor to prescribe them to his/her patients. Don't be bashful about asking your doctor for samples.

3. Begin with a 2-day supply.

Your body may react negatively to a particular drug. So before you fill the entire prescription, try it for a few days. If you need to change drugs after two days, you have only bought the amount you have used. You will not have anymore half full prescription bottles getting wasted. You can buy several pills at a time of any prescription but you must stick with the same pharmacy until that prescription is completed (not including refills).

4. Look for coupons and rebates.

Often a manufacturer will put a coupon on the back of the box or even inside. Check it out before you toss the container.

5. Use generic drugs.

Instead of buying brand name medications, ask your doctor if you can get generic equivalents. This can save you 30% to 50% or more. By federal law, generics have the same amount of active ingredients as brand name drugs. The difference is in the substances used to fill or pack them. You should discuss with your physician the use of generic drugs. Any drug that must maintain a level in you bloodstream i.e. anti-seizure meds, anticoagulants, certain cardiac meds, certain anti-psychotic meds, must be maintained in the form you started. Switching from generic to brand name or vice versa could be fatal.

The active components are the same but your body may react differently with the 'filler' and absorb not enough or too much of the active ingredient in the same dose.

6. Seek cheaper brand name drugs.

If there are no generics available, find out if there are cheaper brand names available.

7. Comparison shop.

Shop around for a pharmacy that offers the best value for your needs. Some drug stores, for example, offer cheaper prices but no services such as home delivery or pharmacist consultations. It may even be worthwhile to compare prices on a prescription-by-prescription basis, since stores sometimes have specials on popular drugs. Have the drug name, dosage and quantity available when you comparison shop.

8. Order online.

Studies show that online pharmacies consistently deliver the lowest overall prices. The next lowest prices are offered by mass merchants such as Wal-Mart, Cosco and Target, followed by supermarkets, independent drug stores and drug chains such as CVS and Walgreens. Although you may be able to save money by ordering on the Internet, you need to exercise caution. Deal with pharmacies that are certified by the National Association of Boards of Pharmacy (NABP). They have developed a system to verify licensure of Internet Pharmacies. Once the pharmacist has met the licensure requirements NABP assigns them a certification of "Verified Internet Pharmacy Practice Site™ (VIPPS)". NABP is located in Park Ridge, Illinois. Their telephone number is (847) 698-6227.

9. Use an online shopping service.

www.pillbot.com will search for the best deal among online pharmacies.

10. Ask your local pharmacy to match the online price.

If you find a cheaper price for your medication on-line, your pharmacist may match the lower price.

11. Check your drugstore's online price.

Some drug stores' online price is as much as 15 percent lower than the pharmacy price.

12. Order by mail.

Mail-order pharmacies now account for 10 to 12 percent of the total prescription market, according to the Pharmaceutical Care Management Association. Ordering by mail, which can save you 10% to 15%, is perfect for patients who take medication on an on-going basis and who can place orders in advance. Some resources that offer discounted mail-order drugs: Medi-Mail, 800-331-1458; and the American Association of Retired Persons (AARP), 800-456-2279.

13. Capitalize on your veteran status.

If you are a veteran, you may be able to get drugs at a very low cost at a Veteran Affairs outpatient clinic.

For more information, go to **www.va.gov** or call 1-877-222-8387.

14. Use over-the-counter drugs.

Some medications that are available without a prescription work as effectively as a prescription and may cost as much as 75 percent less. Some examples of drugs that can be purchased for less than co-pay are antacids, antihistamines and some pain relievers. If you have insurance, make sure you are paying your co-pay on the cheapest amount possible. It may be cheaper to buy the drug without insurance. I know a lady who takes prenatal vitamin tablets. The tablets are covered by her insurance for a $7 co-pay for 30 tablets, or 90 tablets for $21. Since she can buy the tablets over-the-counter and pay $20 for 100 tablets, she has decided not to use her insurance.

15. Get your prescription for a 90-day supply.

If you will be on a drug for a month or more, ask your physician if it is appropriate to order a bulk supply. Some insurance plans allow you to order a 90-day supply for one co-pay.

16. Split pills.

You can get certain prescriptions at double their appropriate dose and then split the tablets in half. Say a pill comes in 50 mg and 100mg. You need 50mg. Ask your doctor to write the prescription for 100 mg and then split the pill. This tactic can result in a 50 percent savings. Consult with your doctor and pharmacist to find out if pill splitting is appropriate for you. Some drugs, such as pills in a time-release formulation, should not be split because you might get a full dose all at once. Also, since pill splitting often results in inexact dosages, your doctor may nix the practice if you need a very precise dose. But if you are given the okay, you can buy a pill splitter to help make the cutting task easier and more accurate.

30

Lower doctors' bills

My doctor gave me six months to live, but when he found out I couldn't pay his bill he gave me six more months.

—Walter Matthau

1. Confirm that your doctor accepts your plan's fees.

Sometimes a doctor's normal fee is more than your plan may cover for a particular medical service. Make sure your doctor is willing to accept the fee that your plan pays.

2. If your primary doctor refers you to a specialist, make sure the specialist is in your plan's network.

Otherwise you get hit with an out-of-network charge.

3. Make sure your doctor uses an "In Network" Lab for blood tests.

Don't assume that your doctor's office knows which labs your plan covers. Have a list of those labs available, and before you leave the doctor's office make sure the nurse knows to send the blood work to a lab covered by your plan.

4. Check each bill for accuracy and for the portion you are responsible for paying.

5. Compare the doctor's bill with the Explanation of Benefits Statement that your insurance company provides.

Make sure the correct code is listed for the service you received.

6. If you go to your doctor regularly, negotiate lower office visit fees.

A few years ago my wife had to go to her doctor's office every week. He graciously agreed to charge her for every other visit.

31

Reduce the cost of a hospital stay

Most hospitals are so expensive that when you go in they should interview you to see which ailment you can afford to have.

—Creative Wit

If you should have to go to the hospital, taking these steps will help you minimize your expenses.

Before going:

1. Make sure you understand your insurance plan's rules.

For example, some policies require you to get preauthorization before being admitted to the hospital for elective surgery. If that is the case, make sure you comply. You will not have to fight for coverage afterwards.

2. Make sure the hospital is in the network.

This will enable you to avoid out-of-network charges.

3. Have routine tests done prior to admission.

Generally, it is less expensive to have such things as blood tests and chest X-rays done as an outpatient.

4. Arrange to have a friend or family member go with you.

It is important to have someone help you keep track of tests you have and medications that you receive. It helps to have this information when it comes time to review your bill for accuracy.

5. Avoid weekend and holiday admission.

Unless your surgery is an emergency, you will not receive much medical care and you will be billed several hundred dollars per day for the room.

While in the hospital:

1. Use your own prescription drugs.

Since hospital pharmacies sometimes charge as much as 200 percent more for drugs than an outside pharmacy, ask your doctor if it is permissible for you to use your own prescription drugs.

2. Keep a diary.

Keep a record of your hospital stay, including the admission date, discharge date, type of room, doctor visits, tests, services and personal items you receive. This information will prove invaluable when it comes to reviewing the charges on your bill after you are released.

3. See if there is a step-down unit.

After a period of time, although you may need less intensive nursing care, you may not be well enough to go home. Most hospitals have what they call a step-down or transitional care unit. Since the cost is significantly less for this service, you can save a lot of money in co-payments.

4. Make sure doctors are in network.

If your primary care physician arranges to have a specialist see you, make sure the specialist is in the network.

5. Check out on time.

Make sure your doctor signs your discharge instructions so you can meet the checkout time (usually 11:00), and thus avoid being billed for an extra day.

At home:

1. Request an itemized bill.

There are three good reasons for wanting to review the bill carefully: 1) the more insurance companies have to pay, the higher premiums they will charge, 2) some insurance companies offer a reward of up to 25 percent of the savings if you find errors, and 3) while auditing 40,000 hospital bills, Equifax Services found that more than 97 percent of the bills contained errors.

2. Look for the most common errors.

Examples are:

a. Double-billing – being charged twice for the same service, medication or supplies.

b. Being billed for services that were never rendered.

c. Incorrect room charge – being billed for a private room when you had a semi-private room.

d. Number of days in the hospital – being billed for the day you checked out.

e. Receiving a generic drug but being charged for a higher priced brand name drug.

f. Being billed for a test that your doctor ordered but later cancelled. Likewise you may have been scheduled for 10 physical, speech or other therapy sessions but received only eight yet got billed for the original 10.

g. Inconsistencies – You have a test on Tuesday and it costs $75. You have the same test on Friday and it costs $125.

h. Having attending doctors' charge on the hospital bill when, in fact, the doctors are rendering you a separate bill.

3. Point out errors.

Call the hospital billing office and point out any errors that you find.

4. Negotiate.

Negotiate a discount in exchange for paying cash. Make sure you talk to the billing supervisor and time your call to arrive at the end of the month/quarter when they are closing the books.

Index

Suggested Reading

Deborah Taylor-Hough, *Frozen Assets: How to Cook for A Day and Eat for A Month*, Champion Press, 2003

Michelle Singletary, *Spend Well, Live Rich,* Ballentine Books, 2004

Deborah Taylor-Hough, *A Simple Choice: A Practical Guide to Saving Your Time*, Money and Sanity, Champion Press, 2000

Thomas Stanley, William Danko, *The Millionaire Next Door*, Pocket, 1998

Jane Bryant Quinn, *Making the Most of Your Money*, Simon & Shuster, 1997

Department of Housing and Urban Development, *100 Questions and Answers About Buying a New Home,* 2003

Federal Trade Commission, *Borrower's Guide to Home Loans,* 2002

Federal Reserve Bank, *Looking for the Best Mortgage: Shop, Compare, Negotiate,* 1999

Department of Agriculture, *How to Buy a Home with a Low Down Payment,* 2001

Department of Housing and Urban Development, *HUD Home Buying Guide,* 2004

Department of Housing and Urban Development, *For Your Protection Get a Home Inspection,* 2005

Federal Trade Commission, *Building A Better Credit Report*, 2005

Federal Trade Commission, *66 Ways to Save Money*, 2004

Insurance Information Institute, *9 Ways to Lower Your Auto Insurance* Costs, 2002

Federal Trade Commission, *How to Get A Great Deal on A New Car*, 2002

Federal Trade Commission, *Buying a Used Car*, 1999

Insurance Information Institute, *12 Ways to Lower Your Homeowner Insurance Costs*, 2003

Federal Citizen Information Center, *What You Should Know About Buying Life Insurance*, 2002

Ronald Kessler, *The Life Insurance Game*, Holt, Rineholt and Winston, 1985

Walter S. Kenton, Jr., *How Life Insurance Companies Rob You*, Random House, 1982

Federal Reserve Bank, *Choosing A Credit Card*, 2002

Department of Energy, *Tips on Saving Energy & Money at Home*, 2003

Gordon Wadsworth, *Cost Effective College,* Moody Press, 2003

Federal Citizen Information Center, *Financial Planning for College*, 2002

Chris Vuturo, *The Scholarship Advisor*, Random House, 1998

Scholarship Resource Network, *The Loan Forgiveness Directory*, 2004

Gail Schlacter and David Webber, *Directory of Financial Aid for Minorities, Reference Service Press,* 1995-1997

U.D. Department of Education, *The Student Guide*, 2005

The author does not assume responsibility for any ideas given. All ideas should be weighed against your own abilities and circumstances and applied accordingly. It is up to you, the reader, to determine if an idea is safe and suitable for your situation.

Printed in the United States
91039LV00002B/550-597/A